Fish in a Flash

Over 200 fast and easy seafood recipes

Charlotte Balcomb Lane

TRIBUNE
PUBLISHING
ORLANDO/1993

Edited by Dixie Kasper
Designed by Karen Harrod Miller

Cover photographs by Tom Burton,
The Orlando Sentinel

Recipe shown: Stir-fried Shrimp with Mangoes (page 89)
Place setting by Mikasa

For information:
Tribune Publishing
P.O. Box 1100
Orlando, Florida 32801

Tribune Publishing

Editorial Director: George C. Biggers III
Managing Editor: Dixie Kasper
Senior Editor: Kathleen M. Kiely
Production Editor: Ken Paskman
Editorial Designer: Bill Henderson

Printed in the United States

First Edition: January, 1993

ISBN 0-941263-55-X

To my parents, Peggy and Ed Balcomb,
whose pleased expressions at the dinner table
hooked me as a teen-ager on cooking.
Without their encouragement and appetites,
I might have gone on to be an orthopedic surgeon
like my sister, Teresa. The whole family is happier
(and healthier) that I took up knife and spatula rather than scalpel.
And to my cat, Kee Kee, whose favorite food is also fish.

Many people have lent their knowledge and expertise to this book
and I thank them. My heartfelt thanks and gratitude go out to
Heather J. McPherson, Betty Boza, Phyllis Gray, David Pratt, Carol Nelson
and Ken Paskman for testing, tasting and making notes on many of the recipes.
My husband, Peter, also deserves thanks for months of patiently
tasting and testing recipes.
For technical advice and expertise, I'd like to thank Clare Vanderbeek
and Emily Holt at the National Fisheries Institute, Tom Thomas at the
Florida Division of Marine Resource and Bureau of Seafood Marketing,
and the editorial staff of *Seafood Leader* and *Simply Seafood* magazines.
Robin Niedz, chief clinical dietitian at Winter Park Memorial Hospital,
provided valuable nutritional information
on the heart-healthy recipes.

A few words about the recipes:

• Substitute one kind of fish for another. Each recipe comes with suggestions, but let your tastes and the availablity of different types of fish and seafood guide you. (See the substitution list on pages 120-121.)

• I love herbs, spices, robust flavors and vibrant seasonings. If you like food a touch milder, adjust the seasonings in the recipes to suit your taste.

• I respect the way a little salt enhances the flavor of food. However, too much salt deadens the flavor. I've tried to use just enough in the recipes to highlight flavors but not overpower the dish.

• Prepared garlic and garlic powder and salt taste overpowering and bitter to me, so I don't use them. I use fresh garlic. I crush it in a garlic press. Professional chefs decry presses but perhaps they don't mind having stinky fingers. A garlic press is fast and convenient.

• Many recipes call for fresh parsley because it adds a wonderful fresh flavor and aroma to every kind of fish and seafood dish. Most grocery stores carry it year-round, it's inexpensive and it keeps

for about two weeks in the refrigerator in a plastic bag with a paper towel.

• For the best flavors, use the best ingredients possible.

These symbols are used throughout the book to help in recipe planning:

 indicates the recipe is low in fat. Oil, butter and saturated fat have been kept to a minimum in developing the recipe, providing a heart-healthy dish.

 indicates there are shortcuts that may be taken in preparing the recipe that won't affect the flavor.

 indicates other types of fish that may be substituted in the recipe.

INTRODUCTION

This book is for people who scan the seafood counter in the grocery store, wishing they had fast, sure-fire recipes. It is for people who love the taste of fish and seafood and enjoy ordering it in restaurants but don't know how to cook it at home.

I was one of those people until I moved to Florida in 1986. Growing up in New Mexico, the closest I got to fresh fish was an occasional Rocky Mountain brook trout my father caught.

In the last few years all that has changed. Advances in processing and transportation have made quality fresh and frozen products available to people all over the country. Fish and seafood departments are becoming mainstays in grocery stores across the country.

Best of all, most of the fish sold at seafood counters is cut into convenient, easy-to-use fillets and steaks. Consumers can enjoy the great flavor and variety of fish and shellfish without having to cut, clean or shuck it themselves. The recipes in this book take advantage of these convenience items to create fast, delicious meals with a minimum of boning and fishy kitchen smells.

Fish and seafood are fast foods. Topped with a delectable sauce or a zesty marinade, most dishes in this book can be prepared in 40 minutes or less. Many can be made ahead and served later. I've tried to simplify, streamline and uncomplicate each recipe so any cook can prepare them, regardless of previous kitchen experience.

The microwave oven, barbecue grill, food processor and blender speed up cooking but do not sacrifice quality. Convenience products such as canned soups, sauces and mixes can do the same.

In Florida, I have learned about the incredible variety of fish and seafood. Some types of fish are delicate, mild and flaky; others are firm, assertive and meaty. Yet, all kinds of fish and seafood are as easy to cook as beef, chicken or pork. The flavors pair well with a cupboard full of ingredients, including citrus juices, nuts, cheeses, mustards and wines. Vibrant flavors such as herbs, garlic, vinegar and olive oil are natural partners for fish and seafood. Plus, fish and seafood dishes are appropriate for any occasion in all seasons.

The American Heart Association and the American Cancer Society urge consumers to eat a balanced diet that includes fish and seafood. Both are good sources of protein and are low in fat. (In this book, recipes that are especially low in fat and calories are marked with a heart symbol.)

Those of us who didn't grow up in Rhode Island or along the Puget Sound can learn to cook fish and seafood as though we did. The 207 recipes in this book are your guide to preparing exquisite fish and seafood in a flash.

How to stock your pantry for cooking fish in a flash

Having these items on hand will speed up cooking and provide you with a range of flavors from which to draw for quick inspiration.

Oils: Virgin olive oil, canola oil, Oriental sesame oil.

Vinegars: Cider vinegar, red and white wine vinegar, sherry vinegar, raspberry vinegar, tarragon vinegar, rice vinegar.

Condiments: Dijon mustard, whole-grain mustard, real mayonnaise, low-calorie or fat-free mayonnaise, Worcestershire sauce, ketchup, lemon juice, liquid hot sauce, prepared horseradish, prepared pesto sauce, anchovy paste, soy sauce, hoisin sauce, Oriental oyster sauce, garlic oil.

Pickles and olives: Sweet pickle relish, pimento-stuffed green olives, pitted black olives, mango chutney, capers.

Pasta and rice: fettuccine, couscous, long grain white rice, Thai jasmine rice or Indian basmati rice, prepared yellow rice mix, broccoli au gratin rice blend, rice vermicelli.

Flours and grains: All-purpose unbleached flour, cornmeal, unseasoned dry bread crumbs, seasoned stuffing mix.

Dried foods: Sun-dried tomatoes, raisins, apricots.

Dried herbs: basil, bay leaves, dill, marjoram, oregano, tarragon, sage, herb blend.

Fresh herbs: Parsley, cilantro, basil, dill, tarragon, marjoram.

Spices: Black and white pepper, ginger, paprika, cayenne pepper or crushed red pepper, curry powder, allspice, nutmeg, cumin, chili powder, lemon pepper, salt.

Nuts: (store in the freezer to keep them fresh) Pecans, almonds, pine nuts, walnuts, unsalted peanuts.

Canned goods: Chicken broth, clam juice, hearts of palm, water-packed tuna, sardines packed in oil, red salmon, tomato paste, whole canned tomatoes, chickpeas, black beans, baby corn.

Frozen foods: Artichoke hearts, chopped spinach, green peas, phyllo dough, puff pastry sheets, fresh bread crumbs, commercially prepared pizza crust, unsalted butter, frozen picked crabmeat, individually frozen fillets, trout fillets.

Refrigerated foods: Low-fat milk, low-fat sour cream, large eggs, low-fat yogurt, Swiss or Gruyere cheese, blue cheese or Gorgonzola, low-fat cream cheese, Parmesan cheese, part-skim mozzarella cheese.

Produce: Garlic, onions, green onions, ginger root, lemons, limes, carrots, celery, potatoes, red or green peppers, roma or plum tomatoes.

CONTENTS

APPETIZERS

Simple and fantastic.

Broiled Oysters with Pesto and Lime

24 oysters on the half shell
1/4 cup pesto sauce, commercial or
   homemade
1 lime
1/4 cup grated Parmesan cheese

 mussels, clams

Preheat oven broiler.

Slip the tip of a sharp knife under each oyster to cut the membrane that attaches the oyster to the shell. This makes it easier to remove the oyster for eating.

Spoon about 1 1/2 teaspoons of the sauce over each oyster. Top with a sprinkling of cheese. Broil about 4 inches from heat source until the oysters are firm and the cheese is brown. Squeeze the fresh lime lightly over each before serving.

Makes 12 servings.

Note: You can also make these using shucked oysters. Cut a long thin loaf of French or sourdough bread into 1/4-inch slices. Place a drained oyster atop each slice. Spoon pesto over oyster and a little around the edges of the bread. Top with cheese. Broil until the oyster is firm and the bread is toasted. Squeeze lime lightly over cooked oysters.

Many Americans are cutting back on the amount of bacon they eat but oysters and bacon are still an unbeatable taste combination. Some people call these Angels on Horseback — I don't know why.

Broiled Oysters with Bacon

24 large oysters, drained
8 slices of bacon

Cut the bacon into thirds. Wrap each oyster with bacon and secure with a toothpick. Place in a single layer on a baking sheet.

Preheat oven to 375 F. Bake for 10 minutes, until bacon is brown and oyster is firm. You may need to turn them to ensure even cooking. Drain and serve hot.

Makes 24 appetizers.

An outstanding combination of sweet, salty and toothsome. The dates almost become creamy as they cook.

Bacon, Shrimp and Date Rumaki

24 medium shrimp, peeled and
    deveined
12 whole pitted dates
8 slices of bacon

Slice the dates in half lengthwise. Slice the bacon into thirds. Press the date half against the side of each shrimp and wrap a piece of bacon around both. Secure with a toothpick or a short bamboo skewer.

Preheat oven to 375 F. Bake in a single layer on a baking sheet. Bake for 6 minutes and flip each appetizer over. Bake 6 more minutes, or until bacon is crisp and shrimp are curled. Blot to remove excess grease. Serve hot.

Makes 24 appetizers.

Green lip mussels are farm-raised mollusks from New Zealand that have exquisite green shells and magnificent, salmon-colored flesh. They're about twice the size of ordinary blue-black mussels. They're often sold on the half shell.

Broiled Green Lip Mussels with Red Pepper Mayonnaise

36 green lip mussels
1/3 cup Red Pepper Mayonnaise
(recipe page 196)

 farm-raised East Coast mussels, oysters, clams

If the mussels are unopened, insert the blade of a knife between the shells at the hinge. Twist the blade and pop the shells open. Discard one half of the shell and arrange the opened shells and meat upright on a baking sheet.

Preheat oven broiler. Spoon about 1 1/2 teaspoons of Red Pepper Mayonnaise over each mussel. Broil about 4 inches from the heat source for 2 to 4 minutes, or until the mayonnaise is 4bubbling and browned.

Makes 6 servings.

Note: Of domestic varieties, Penn Cove Mussels, a farm-raised variety from Coupeville, Wash., are some of the best I have tasted. Not a speck of sand.

A fresh and refreshing alternative to shrimp cocktail. Savor any leftover Lemon Relish with cream cheese and crackers or plain baked fish.

Tuna Cocktail
With Avocado and Lemon Relish

2 (6-ounce) fresh tuna fillets
2 tablespoons parsley
2 tablespoons red onion, minced
1/4 cup dry white wine
1/4 teaspoon freshly ground black
   pepper
1/4 teaspoon salt
1 small avocado, diced into 1/4-inch
   cubes (about 1 cup)
1 cup shredded lettuce
Lemon Relish (recipe follows)

 swordfish, shark,
halibut, sea scallops

Cut the tuna into 1/4-inch pieces. Combine the tuna, parsley, red onion, wine, pepper and salt in a microwave-safe serving dish. Allow to marinate refrigerated for 20 minutes to 1 hour.

Cover loosely with plastic wrap. Cook on high (100 percent) power for 3 to 4 minutes, until fish is opaque and firm to the touch. Allow to cool in marinade and then refrigerate for at least 20 minutes. When ready to serve, divide lettuce into four portions.

Combine tuna and marinade ingredients with cubed avocado and mound on top of shredded lettuce.

Serve topped with a dollop of Lemon Relish.

Makes 6 servings.

Lemon Relish

1/2 cup lemon rind, diced (about 4
    lemons, peeled)
2 tablespoons olive oil
1 cup sweet onion, such as Vidalia,
    Florida or Walla Walla
6 tablespoons sugar
1/4 cup white wine or vermouth
2 lemons, peeled, seeded and diced
    (about 1/3 cup pulp)
1/4 teaspoon salt
1/4 teaspoon white pepper

Remove the yellow part of the rind from lemons, trying to include as little as possible of the white pith, which can be bitter.

Combine the yellow rind, olive oil and onions in a saucepan over medium-low heat. Cook slowly, stirring occasionally, until the onions are soft and transparent, about 10 minutes. Add the sugar, wine, lemon pulp, salt and pepper. Simmer over medium-low heat until mixture begins to look glossy, about 10 to 12 minutes.

Remove from heat and allow to cool.

Chill until ready to serve. To serve, spoon 1 tablespoon over Tuna Cocktail and pass remaining relish separately.

Makes 8 servings.

Note: Relish will keep for several months in a tightly closed jar in the refrigerator. It can also be frozen. Serve leftover Lemon Relish with any kind of fish or with cream cheese and crackers.

Rock shrimp are little crustaceans from Florida. They are members of the shrimp family but look and taste like miniature lobsters. The sweet, chewy flesh is often removed from the tough shell and sold ready to eat.

Rock Shrimp Croquettes

1 medium baking potato (about 8 ounces)
1/2 pound rock shrimp, shelled and cooked
4 green onions, diced (about 1/2 cup)
1/4 cup finely chopped fresh parsley
1 tablespoon Dijon-style mustard
1/4 teaspoon salt
1 teaspoon lemon juice
1/8 teaspoon cayenne pepper
1/8 teaspoon black pepper
1/8 teaspoon thyme
1/8 teaspoon nutmeg
2 egg whites
1/8 teaspoon cream of tartar
1 cup peanut oil

 regular shrimp, lobster tail, crawfish

Wash the potato and prick it with a fork. Cover and cook in a microwave oven on high (100 percent power) for 7 to 8 minutes, turning over once. Allow to cool. Peel and mash the potato and place in a medium bowl.

Chop the rock shrimp until they are the size of peas. Add them to the bowl with the potato, green onions, mustard, salt, lemon juice, cayenne pepper, black pepper, parsley, thyme and nutmeg. Mash ingredients with a spatula until well mixed and sticky enough to hold together.

In another bowl, beat egg whites and cream of tartar on high speed until stiff. Egg whites should not slide when bowl is tilted. Fold the egg whites into the shrimp mixture. Mixture should be fluffy not soupy. Heat the oil in a non-stick skillet over medium heat. Oil should be hot before adding shrimp mixture. Using a tablespoon, drop the croquette mixture into the hot oil. Brown on one side, about 5 minutes, until croquette is firm enough to turn without breaking. Do not turn before mixture is set. Cook on second side for 3 minutes, or until brown and crispy. Keep warm in a 250-degree oven while cooking remaining croquettes. Serve hot with Pepper Jelly Sauce (recipe follows) or sweet mustard.

Makes 18 appetizers.

Note: These can be prepared in advance, frozen and reheated on a lightly oiled baking sheet. Allow the croquettes to crisp in the oven for about 10 minutes before serving. Do not allow them to become dry.

Pepper Jelly Sauce

1/4 cup hot pepper jelly or jalapeno
   pepper jelly (available in most
   grocery stores or gourmet shops)
1 tablespoon white-wine vinegar
1 tablespoon white wine

In a microwave-safe dish, melt the
pepper jelly on high (100 percent power).
Stir in vinegar and wine. Allow to cool
slightly.
   Makes 1/3 cup.

*Assemble the ingredients in advance and slip them under the broiler just before sitting
down to eat. Double the recipe to make dinner portions.*

Broiled Scampi

24 jumbo shrimp, peeled
Juice of 1 lemon, about 3 tablespoons
1 stick unsalted butter
2 cloves garlic, peeled
2 tablespoons finely chopped fresh
   parsley
1/4 cup dry white wine or vermouth
1/8 teaspoon white pepper
Fresh French or Italian bread

 scallops, lobster medallions

   Butterfly the shrimp by slicing through
the backs from tip to tail. Remove the
dark vein, if there is one.
   Divide the shrimp between 4 individual ramekins or oven-proof serving
dishes. Place the tails together in the
center for a pretty presentation. In a food
processor, combine the garlic, butter,
pepper and parsley. Puree until smooth
and fluffy. Divide the butter between each
serving. Divide the lemon juice, and
wine or vermouth between each dish.
Refrigerate until ready to serve.
   Preheat oven broiler. Broil each dish
for 4 minutes, or until shrimp are pink,
curled and sizzling.
   Allow dishes to stand for about 2
minutes to cool slightly. Shrimp will
continue to cook. Use bread for soaking
up the garlic butter.
   Makes 4 servings.

Soft-shell crabs used to be a seasonal rarity. Now, they are available frozen almost year-round. In this recipe, the raspberry flavor is exquisite with the sweet crab meat.

Sauteed Soft-Shell Crabs with Raspberry Butter

6 soft-shell crabs, thawed and well-drained if frozen
1/2 cup flour
1/4 teaspoon salt
1/8 teaspoon white pepper
4 tablespoons butter
2 tablespoons olive oil
4 tablespoons raspberry vinegar
Parsley or fresh raspberries for garnish

soft-shell crawfish

Rinse crabs under running water. In a shallow plate, combine the flour, salt and pepper. Dredge the crabs in the flour to coat evenly. Shake off the excess.

In a large skillet over medium-high heat, combine the butter and olive oil. When the butter starts to foam, add the crabs to the pan, leaving plenty of space between each. (You may need to cook the crabs in 2 batches or in 2 pans.) Cook for 4 to 5 minutes per side, depending on size. Crabs should be golden brown. Remove to serving plates and garnish with parsley or raspberries.

Pour the raspberry vinegar in the hot pan, stirring constantly. Bring to a boil, scraping up the browned bits off the bottom of the pan. Cook for 2 minutes. Pour a little of the raspberry liquid over each crab. Serve hot garnished with parsley or fresh raspberries.

Makes 6 servings.

Note: Soft-shell crabs are in the molting phase between shedding their old shells and growing new ones. Most are sold ready to eat, frozen or thawed, in seafood markets.

This yummy fish spread is typical of Florida's Gulf Coast. It's also great served with crackers and heaped in celery sticks.

Crepe Pinwheels
With Smoked Fish Pate

1 1/2 pounds smoked fish such as mullet, amberjack or snapper, flaked
2 tablespoons onion, minced
2 tablespoons celery, minced
2 tablespoons minced sweet pickle or pickle relish
2 tablespoons minced fresh parsley
1 tablespoon Dijon-style mustard
1 cup light mayonnaise
1/4 teaspoon Worcestershire sauce
Crepes (recipe follows)

Mix all ingredients together. Mixture should be thick and creamy. Refrigerate.

Spread each crepe with cup of filling. Roll crepes into tight pinwheels. Slice into small rounds. Serve chilled.

Makes 3 cups.

Make the smoked fish pate up to 3 days in advance and store in the refrigerator. The crepes can be made up to 1 month in advance and frozen. Use wax paper to separate the crepes.

Crepes

1/2 cup flour
1/4 teaspoon salt
1/4 teaspoon dill
2 eggs, lightly beaten
1/2 cup milk

Combine the flour, salt and dill in a large bowl. Beat together eggs and milk. Stir into flour to make a thin batter. Refrigerate for 30 minutes or overnight. Spray a non-stick 6-inch skillet with cooking spray or coat lightly with oil.

Pour in 1/4 cup of crepe batter and tilt pan to coat bottom. Cook for 1 to 2 minutes, turn and cook for 30 seconds longer. Stack on waxed paper; allow to cool.

Makes 12 crepes.

Note: If desired, season the batter with 1/4 teaspoon of an herb such as dill, tarragon or basil.

This recipes is patterned after Spanish recipes for tapas, small afternoon or early evening snacks designed to be eaten with drinks. Spear the shrimp with toothpicks and sop up the flavorful oil with good bread.

Shrimp in Garlic Oil

1 pound medium to large shrimp, shelled and deveined

1 teaspoon salt

2 cups ice water

1/3 cup olive oil

2 cloves of garlic, minced or crushed through a press

1/4 teaspoon crushed red pepper flakes

1 tablespoon dry sherry

1 teaspoon red wine vinegar

3 tablespoons finely chopped fresh parsley

 scallops, squid, mussels

In a bowl, combine the salt and ice water. Stir to dissolve the salt. Soak the shrimp for 5 minutes. Drain and pat dry.

In a large non-stick skillet, heat the olive oil. Add the shrimp without crowding. (Cook two batches if necessary.) Stir in the garlic and the red pepper. Add the sherry, vinegar and parsley and cook for about 2 to 3 minutes, until the shrimp are pink and curled. Transfer shrimp and cooking juices to a dish and serve with sourdough bread.

Makes 8 servings.

Cabbage and smoked fish blend wonderfully with the nutty flavor of walnuts. Vegetables add freshness and crunch. This recipe is delicious but fairly labor intensive. Make it ahead of time and heat before serving.

Smoked Fish and Walnut Cabbage Rolls

1 cup smoked fish, such as kingfish, sable, mullet or trout

1 head Napa (Chinese) cabbage or savoy cabbage (about 1 pound)

1/2 pound fresh spinach leaves, washed and drained

1 tablespoon canola oil

1 clove garlic, crushed through a press

1 small carrot, cut into thin, 2-inch strips

1 small zucchini, cut into thin, 2-inch strips

3 small green onions, cut into thin, 2-inch strips

1 cup chopped walnuts

1/8 teaspoon freshly ground black pepper

1 1/2 tablespoons low-sodium soy sauce

1/2 cup clam juice or chicken broth

1 tablespoon cornstarch dissolved in 2 tablespoons of water

1 cup bean sprouts

Preheat oven to 350 degrees.

Crumble the smoked fish and remove any bones or skin. Set aside.

Gently peel off 8 outer leaves from the cabbage and blanch in boiling water about 4 minutes or until barely wilted. Remove from water, drain and allow to cool. Set aside. Shred remaining cabbage until you have 2 cups.

Trim stems off spinach. Shred and set aside.

In a wok or large, heavy-bottomed skillet heat the oil over medium-high heat. Stir in garlic, carrot, zucchini and green onions and saute until onions and carrots are tender, about 4 to 5 minutes. Add the spinach, soy sauce, clam juice. Bring the liquid to a boil and stir in the cornstarch mixture. Mixture should thicken as soon as the liquid returns to a boil. Remove from heat.

Stir in bean sprouts, smoked fish and walnuts.

Divide mixture among 8 blanched cabbage leaves. Roll up leaves lengthwise to enclose vegetables. Place, folded side down, in a shallow ovenproof casserole. Pour any remaining juices over rolls. Bake 5 minutes or until heated through.

If desired, top with sour cream or imitation sour cream.

Makes 4 appetizer servings.

The arid Southwest never saw an oyster until recently — but the shellfish taste great with a spicy topping of salsa and cheese!

Southwestern Broiled Oysters

24 oysters in the shell
1/2 cup commercial salsa
1 (6-inch) corn tortilla
1/4 cup finely chopped fresh cilantro
3/4 cup grated Monterey Jack cheese

Scrub the outside of the oyster shells under running water with a stiff brush. Use an oyster knife to pry open the shells and loosen the membranes that hold the oyster in place. Place the oysters on the half shell on a baking sheet. If the oysters tip and rock, line the baking sheet with crumpled aluminum foil. Foil will form a bed for oysters.

Tear the corn tortilla into tiny bits. Grind it in a blender or food processor with the cilantro. Add the salsa. Spoon about 1 teaspoon of the mixture over each oyster and top with cheese.

Preheat broiler. Cook about 4 inches from the heat for 3 to 5 minutes, or until cheese is browned and melted.

Makes 8 servings.

The flavor of corn tortilla chips is exquisite with oysters.

Oyster Nachos

1 (12-ounce) container shucked
   oysters
1/2 cup commercial salsa
1 (6-inch) corn tortilla
1/4 cup finely chopped fresh cilantro
3/4 cup grated Monterey Jack cheese

Tear the corn tortilla into tiny bits. Grind it in a blender or food processor with the cilantro. Add the salsa. Set aside.

Drain shucked oysters throughly. Place each on a tostada chip, top with salsa mixture and cheese and broil until cheese melts.

Watch carefully to prevent the chips from burning.

Makes about 24 nachos.

Oyster tips:

• Oysters cook very quickly. They are done as soon as the meat is firm and the edges curl. Do not overcook them or they will taste musky and tough.

• It is safe to eat oysters year-round. The old advice about avoiding oysters during months without an "R" is out of date. Oysters spawn during the warm summer months and lose their flavor. However, modern seafood markets can buy oysters from cold waters and get firm, fresh specimens even in June, July and August.

• Avoid eating raw oysters.

Shucking oysters:

• Use an oyster knife. The blade is strong and pointed and has a guard at the handle.
• Scrub the oyster under cold, running water to keep from getting sand inside the shell.
• Wrap a dishcloth around the hand holding the shell to keep from cutting yourself if the blade should slip.
• Insert the knife blade between the shells at the hinge end. Twist until you hear the halves separate.
• Pull the shells apart and slide the blade under the oyster to cut the membrane. Remove any bits of shell.
• The oyster is ready to use in recipes.

This lovely pink and red hors d'oeuvre spread is perfect for a wedding shower or a Valentine's Day party.

Salmon Caviar Spread

1 (15-ounce) can red salmon, drained
1 tablespoon whole grain mustard
3 ounces cream cheese, softened
1/4 cup sour cream or imitation sour
   cream
1 clove garlic
4 drops liquid hot sauce
1/2 teaspoon dill
2 tablespoons lemon juice
3 tablespoons red caviar
Parsley for garnish

 smoked salmon

Pick through salmon and remove bones and skin. Discard. Flake meat and set aside.

In a blender or food processor, combine the mustard, cream cheese, sour cream, garlic, hot sauce, lemon juice and dill. Blend until smooth. Transfer the cream mixture to a bowl and gently fold in the salmon and caviar. Pack into a serving container and chill thoroughly. Garnish with parsley and serve with sliced sourdough bread, crackers or toast points.

Makes 2 cups.

Note: One 2-ounce jar of red lumpfish caviar yields about 3 tablespoons, with just enough left to make a pretty garnish for the top.

This is an easy way to show off the flavor of oysters.

Oyster Tarts

20 oysters, shucked
1 roll refrigerated biscuit dough (10 giant biscuits)
2 green onions, finely minced
3 tablespoons sesame seeds

 smoked oysters, shelled mussels, scallops

Drain oysters. Place on a paper towel.

On a work surface, separate biscuits. Pull each biscuit in half to make two thin biscuits. Press into the cups of two mini-muffin tins. Top each with green onions and an oyster. Pull dough over the oyster and pinch to seal or form cups. Sprinkle with sesame seeds.

Preheat oven to 400 F. Bake for 12 to 13 minutes until biscuits are golden brown. Serve hot with Sesame Hoisin Sauce.

Makes 20.

Note: These should be made right before serving.

Sesame Hoisin Sauce

1/4 cup hoisin sauce
1 tablespoon soy sauce
1 tablespoon lemon juice
1 tablespoon rice vinegar
1 teaspoon Oriental sesame oil

Stir all ingredients to combine well. Makes 1/2 cup.

Note: Hoisin sauce is a pungent Oriental condiment made of soybean paste, garlic and other ingredients. It's available in most supermarkets and in Oriental markets.

The Belgian people are very fond of mussels. When I lived in Antwerp in the 1970s as a foreign exchange student, every pub and cafe served a variation on steamed mussels. I make this version with beer, the Belgian national beverage.

Belgian-Style Steamed Mussels

4 pounds mussels in the shells
1 small yellow onion, chopped (about 1/2 cup)
1/4 cup chopped fresh parsley
1 cup beer
1 cup water
2 tablespoons lemon juice
4 tablespoons (1/2 stick) unsalted butter
French bread

Rinse the mussels under running water and pull off the beards if still attached. Discard any mussels that are open.

In a stainless steel kettle or large enameled tea pot, combine the onion, parsley, beer, water, lemon juice and butter. Bring mixture to a rolling boil.

Add mussels to liquid. Cover and bring liquid back to a boil, shaking pan occasionally. Cook for 5 to 7 minutes. Remove from heat.

Use a slotted spoon to remove mussels to 4 serving bowls and reserve liquid. Discard any mussels that have not opened. Bring mixture back to a boil and boil uncovered for 5 minutes, until slightly reduced in volume. Pour hot liquid over the mussels and serve with bread for dunking.

Makes 4 servings.

Note: If a mussel feels very heavy for its size, it may be full of sand. Discard it. If you like a spicy flavor, add a dash or two of hot pepper sauce.

Smoked Oyster Turnovers

1 (6-ounce) can smoked oysters in oil
1 stalk celery, very finely diced
1 sheet ready-made frozen puff pastry, thawed
1 egg beaten with 1 tablespoon milk

Preheat oven to 325 F.

Drain the oysters and set aside. Cut any extra-large oysters in half.

Lightly flour a board and roll the sheet of puff pastry until it is 1/8 inch thick. Use a 1 1/2 inch-diameter cookie cutter to cut the dough into circles. Remove excess dough and save for another purpose.

Brush each circle lightly with the egg-milk mixture. Place one smoked oyster and about 1/2 teaspoon of diced celery on each circle. Fold pastry over and press with your fingertips to seal.

Transfer to a cookie sheet that has been lined with parchment paper. Bake for 10 to 12 minutes until each turnover is puffed and browned. Serve hot.

Makes about 24 turnovers.

These delicious Pecan-Crusted Fish Fingers with Fiesty Apricot Sauce are wonderful party appetizers. The recipe doubles or triples easily to serve a crowd. They're also great for light meals, rounded out with a salad or a vegetable.

Pecan-Crusted Fish Fingers

1 pound firm fish, such as snapper
1/2 teaspoon paprika
1/2 teaspoon onion powder
1/4 teaspoon cayenne pepper
1/4 teaspoon white pepper or freshly ground black pepper
1/4 teaspoon ground thyme
1/4 teaspoon cumin
1/4 teaspoon salt
1/4 cup pecan meal or 1/2 cup pecan halves
1 egg white
2 teaspoons canola oil

 mahi mahi, shark, tuna, swordfish, sturgeon, striped bass

Slice the fish into strips about 1-inch wide and 2 to 3 inches long. Set aside.

Beat the egg white lightly in a wide shallow dish. In another dish, thoroughly mix together the spices, seasonings and pecan meal. (If using pecan halves, grind nuts until they are the consistency of coffee grounds.)

Dip each fish finger in the egg white then roll lightly in the pecan-spice mixture. Set aside on a sheet of wax paper. If not cooking immediately, refrigerate uncovered. (You can prepare the fingers up to several hours in advance at this point.)

Heat the canola oil in a large, shallow non-stick skillet over medium-high heat. Cook the fish fingers without crowding, turning occasionally with a spatula. Be careful not to break the fish. Cook until the fish is firm to the touch and the pecan meal is golden brown, about 5 to 7 minutes. If the pecan meal browns too quickly, turn down the heat.

Drain lightly on paper towels. Serve warm with Fiesty Apricot Sauce (recipe follows).

Makes 12 fingers or 6 servings.

Notes: Pecan meal is available in many grocery stores or where fresh in-shell pecans are sold. If you can't find it, grind pecan pieces or halves in a coffee grinder or food processor until the mixture is fine but not oily.

If desired, substitute a Cajun spice mixture or blackening blend for spices and seasonings called for in this recipe. Look for brands that are low in sodium.

Fiesty Apricot Sauce

1 cup canned apricot nectar
2 tablespoons prepared Creole mustard (may substitute whole-grain mustard)
1 tablespoon cider vinegar
1 tablespoon cornstarch

In a small saucepan, combine the apricot nectar and the Creole mustard. Stir to blend and bring to a boil over medium heat.

In a small dish, combine the vinegar and cornstarch and stir to make a paste. When the nectar boils, stir in the cornstarch mixture. Stir until the mixture thickens. Remove from heat and serve warm or at room temperature.

Makes 1 1/4 cups or 12 servings.

Notes: For a spicier version of this sauce, add 1/4 teaspoon of cayenne pepper to the nectar and mustard mixture. For a milder version, use plain mustard instead of the spicy variety. Mango or peach nectar is also good in this recipe.

Creole mustard is a blend of brown and white mustards, with vinegar and other seasonings. Several brands are available in grocery stores. If unavailable, substitute hot mustard or whole-grain mustard.

SALADS

Snow crab has an exquisite, sweet flavor. It's highlighted in this luxurious salad of fresh, colorful ingredients.

Deviled Crab Salad on Artichoke Bottoms

16 ounces frozen Canadian snow crab meat, thawed
2 stalks celery, finely chopped
1 small red or green bell pepper (about 1 cup), finely chopped
1 green onion, finely chopped
3 tablespoons chopped fresh parsley
3 tablespoons whole-grain mustard or Dijon mustard
6 tablespoons mayonnaise
1 tablespoon lemon juice
Pinch sugar
Freshly ground black pepper
4 dashes hot sauce
1 (15-ounce) can artichoke bottoms packed in brine
Lettuce leaves

Pick through the crab meat to remove any bits of cartilage or shell. In a large bowl, combine it with the celery, red or green bell pepper, green onion and parsley. In a small bowl, combine the mustard, mayonnaise, lemon juice, sugar and hot sauce. Fold into the crab salad. Top with a sprinkling of black pepper.

Drain the artichoke bottoms. Pile the salad in the artichokes and place atop lettuce leaves. If desired, garnish with sliced cucumbers, radishes, hearts of palm or artichoke hearts.

Makes 4 to 6 servings.

Note: Salad may exude moisture but that doesn't affect the flavor.

imitation crab, canned crab, cooked shrimp, cooked fish, canned salmon

Prepare the salad and the dressing separately up to 2 days in advance and combine them a few hours before serving. Place them in the artichoke bottoms up to an hour in advance.

Boiling the liquid the shrimp and asparagus have poached in concentrates the flavors in this remarkable Spanish-style salad. It's an ideal salad to serve in April and May when asparagus is in season.

Warm Shrimp, Asparagus and Ham Salad

16 extra-large shrimp
1 1/2 pounds asparagus
1 (8-ounce) bottle clam juice
1 tablespoon lemon juice
2 ounces country ham, sliced into thin strips
2 tablespoons olive oil
2 cloves garlic, crushed through a press
2 tablespoons sherry vinegar

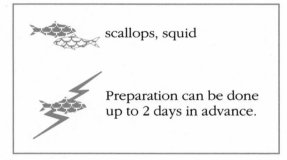

scallops, squid

Preparation can be done up to 2 days in advance.

Break the ends off the asparagus at the point where they snap easily. Rinse under cold water and cut on the diagonal into 2-inch pieces. Set aside.

Combine the clam juice and lemon juice in a shallow saucepan. Bring to a boil. Add the shrimp. When the liquid returns to a boil, reduce heat to a simmer and cook for 3 to 5 minutes until shrimp are pink and the tails curl. Use a slotted spoon to remove from the liquid. Spread the shrimp out on a plate to cool. Peel.

Add the asparagus to the liquid and cook for 3 to 4 minutes, until the stalks are bright green but tender. Remove the asparagus with a slotted spoon and spread out on a plate to cool. The cooking liquid should have reduced to 2 tablespoons; if not, boil a minute longer until it does. Set aside.

The recipe can be prepared ahead to this point. If the recipe is prepared more than 1 hour in advance, refrigerate all the ingredients until ready to finish cooking.

Heat the oil in a large skillet. Add the ham and fry for 3 to 4 minutes, until it starts to brown. Add the garlic, cooking liquid and sherry vinegar. Bring to a vigorous boil. Add the shrimp and asparagus and cook just long enough to heat through. Divide on four plates. Serve with warm bread, if desired. Excellent served warm or cold.

Makes 4 servings.

Note: Sherry vinegar is aged in wooden casks so it has a smooth, nutty flavor. You can substitute balsamic, red wine or cider vinegar, but decrease the amount used to 1 tablespoon.

A salad that captures the flavors of summer – even in December.

Tuna, White Bean and Pasta Salad

8 ounces rotini (twists) or penne pasta, cooked according to package directions
3/4 cup Sara's Honey Balsamic Vinegar Dressing (recipe page 197), divided
1/2 teaspoon salt
1 (16-ounce) can cannellini or Great Northern beans, rinsed and drained
1 (7-ounce) can tuna, packed in water and drained
9 ounces frozen green beans, thawed (or 2 cups fresh)
1/4 cup fresh parsley, minced

fresh cooked tuna, cooked swordfish, cooked mahi mahi

Make the dressing up to 1 week in advance.

Cook the pasta until tender but not mushy. Drain well and pour 1/2 cup of the dressing over the hot pasta. Add salt and toss well to coat evenly.

Combine the white beans and tuna with the pasta. (If using fresh green beans, cook in boiling salted water for 8 minutes, or until tender but still slightly crunchy. Drain and rinse with cold water to stop the cooking. Drain and add to the pasta mixture.) If using frozen beans, cook 2 minutes in a microwave oven on high (100 percent) power. Cool and add to pasta mixture. Toss salad with parsley and remaining dressing. Refrigerate until ready to serve.

Makes 8 servings.

Note: If desired, add 1 cup of chopped fresh basil or 1 teaspoon dried basil to the salad. Like all pasta salads, this one absorbs a vast amount of dressing. If you have leftovers, it may be a good idea to toss the pasta with about 1/3 cup more dressing before serving.

Caesar salads are almost universally popular. The grilled fish makes a good thing even better.

Warm Caesar Salad
with Grilled Halibut or Salmon

1 pound halibut or salmon steaks
1 tablespoon canola oil
3 canned anchovy fillets or
   1/2 teaspoon anchovy paste
1 large clove garlic, peeled and
   crushed through a press
3 tablespoons olive oil
3 tablespoons lemon juice
1/4 cup freshly grated Parmesan
   cheese, divided
1 tablespoon Dijon-style mustard
1/4 teaspoon freshly ground black
   pepper
1 head romaine lettuce, torn into bite-
   sized pieces
1 cup Buttered Croutons (recipe
   page 202)

Heat a barbecue grill to medium-high. Brush the halibut or salmon steaks with the oil. Cook 6 to 8 minutes on each side, depending on thickness. Fish should be firm to the touch, but not appear dry on the surface. Remove from heat and keep warm.

Mash the anchovies with a fork in the bottom of a large salad bowl. Add the olive oil, lemon juice, garlic, 2 table-spoons of the Parmesan cheese and the mustard to the mixture. Add the lettuce, croutons and remaining Parmesan cheese and toss well to coat every leaf. Divide among four salad plates.

Remove the skin and bones from the fish. Cut into chunks and arrange over the salads. Pour any accumulated fish juice over the lettuce as well.

Makes 4 servings.

Note: You can also use Sara's Honey Balsamic Vinegar Dressing instead of the Caesar dressing.

striped bass, swordfish, shark

Grill the fish and make the dressing in advance. Serve the salad chilled or at room temperature.

Thai Rice and Shrimp Salad with Peanut Dressing

4 cups cooked white or brown rice, cooled

1 cup cooked baby shrimp or 2 cups large shrimp, cooked and coarsely chopped

1 cucumber, peeled and diced

1 sweet red bell pepper, seeded and diced

2 green onions, chopped

4 cups shredded lettuce or fresh spinach

Dressing:

1/3 cup chunky peanut butter

1/4 cup cider vinegar

2 tablespoons canola or peanut oil

2 tablespoons soy sauce

1 tablespoon brown sugar

1 teaspoon fresh, chopped ginger

1 clove garlic, crushed through a press

Pinch crushed red pepper (optional)

3 tablespoons water

In a mixing bowl, combine the cooked rice, shrimp, cucumber, red pepper and green onions.

In a microwave-safe dish, combine the peanut butter, vinegar, oil, soy sauce, brown sugar, ginger, garlic, crushed red pepper and water. Cook on high (100 percent) power for 1 minute. Stir and cook for 1 minute longer or until peanut butter is melted and the dressing is smooth. Pour the dressing over the shrimp and rice salad. Toss to coat evenly. Serve on a bed of shredded lettuce or spinach.

Makes 4 main-course servings or 6 appetizer servings.

Note: Frozen cooked baby shrimp are available in one-pound bags in the frozen food department of most grocery stores. The package will yield about 4 cups ready-to-use shrimp.

scallops

Use cooked, shelled and deveined shrimp, which are available frozen in most grocery stores.

A fresh, light and appealing salad for a summer luncheon.

Shrimp and Watermelon Salad

3 cups watermelon balls, seeded
2 tablespoons fresh lime juice
2 cups frozen baby shrimp, thawed
3 green onions, chopped
1 small yellow or green bell pepper, seeded and diced
1/3 cup pecan pieces
1/4 cup chopped fresh parsley
Leaf lettuce

Dressing:
1/2 cup plain low-fat yogurt
1/4 cup mayonnaise
2 tablespoons whole-grain or Dijon mustard
1 tablespoon lime or lemon juice
1 clove garlic, crushed through a press
1/2 teaspoon dried tarragon or 4 tablespoons fresh tarragon
1/4 teaspoon salt

In a mixing bowl, combine the watermelon and shrimp. Sprinkle evenly with lime juice. Add pepper, pecan and parsley. Toss gently to combine. Line a bowl or individual serving plates with lettuce and mound salad in the center.

Mix all the ingredients for the dressing. Spoon over salad just before serving.

Makes 6 servings

Notes: A 4 1/4 pound seedless baby watermelon will yield exactly 3 cups of melon balls, made with the small end of a double-scoop melon baller. Baby shrimp are usually sold precooked. To heat them, drop them in boiling water for less than 1 minute. Remove them with a slotted spoon.

This marinated seafood salad is so good it deserves to be served for a party. But you don't have to save it for a special occasion.

Marinated Squid Salad

1 pound cleaned squid, sliced into rings

2 tablespoons olive oil

4 roma tomatoes, seeded and diced

1/3 cup red onion, diced

8 black pitted olives, sliced into rings

1/4 cup fresh chopped parsley

1/2 teaspoon basil or 4 tablespoons fresh chopped basil

Vinaigrette Dressing:

1/2 cup canola or peanut oil or 1/4 cup each olive oil and salad oil

1 large clove garlic, crushed through a press

1/4 cup cider or white wine vinegar

2 tablespoons whole-grain or Dijon-style mustard

1/4 teaspoon salt

1/4 teaspoon sugar

1/4 teaspoon freshly ground black pepper

Combine all the ingredients for the dressing in a jar with a tight-fitting lid. Shake well to blend. Set aside.

In a large, non-stick skillet, heat the 2 tablespoons olive oil. Cook the squid over medium-high heat without crowding for 2 to 3 minutes, until opaque. Immediately pour squid and cooking juices into a serving bowl. Do not overcook or the squid will be tough. Pour dressing over squid and add the chopped tomatoes, red onion, olives, parsley and basil.

Toss well. Refrigerate and allow the squid to marinate for at least 1 hour. Serve chilled.

Makes 4 servings.

shrimp, scallops, mussels or tuna

Have the fish market clean the squid for you.

The spiciness of curry and the sweetness of crab are complementary flavors.

Curried Crab and Apple Salad

**1 pound crab meat, shell and
  cartilage removed**
**1 large tart green apple, such as
  Granny Smith, cored**
1 stalk celery, diced (about 1 cup)
1 carrot, shredded (about 1/2 cup)
1 green onion, finely chopped

Dressing:
2 heaping teaspoons curry powder
2 tablespoons mayonnaise
1 tablespoon lemon juice
1/2 cup plain low-fat yogurt
Dash hot pepper sauce (optional)

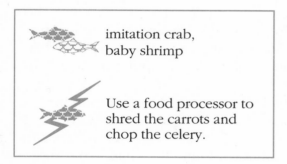

imitation crab,
baby shrimp

Use a food processor to
shred the carrots and
chop the celery.

Dice the apple and combine it with the crab meat or imitation crab. Add the celery, carrot and green onion. Stir in the ingredients for the dressing and combine well.

Refrigerate until ready to serve.

Makes 6 luncheon servings or 4 main dish servings.

Notes: This is pretty when served in an edible bowl of half of a fresh cantaloupe or ripe papaya, or atop a wedge of pine-apple. It also can be mounded in tomato cups for a luncheon presentation. Garnish with freshly roasted and chopped almonds, if desired.

Pastel colors and a terrific flavor make this a year-round favorite.

Salmon Raspberry Salad
in Avocado Cups

**1 pound fresh salmon fillet or 1 (15-
   ounce) can red salmon**
1 cucumber, peeled, seeded and diced
1/2 pint fresh raspberries
4 tablespoons canola oil
4 tablespoons raspberry vinegar
1/4 teaspoon dried basil
2 ripe avocados

 shrimp, cooked sword-
fish, halibut, mahi mahi,
cod or scallops

If using fresh salmon, remove any bones and place in a microwave-safe baking dish. Cover with waxed paper and cook on medium (50 percent) power for 4 minutes. Turn fish over and cook on medium (50 percent) power for 3 to 4 minutes longer, until fish is firm to the touch. Allow to stand for 5 minutes. Flake fish and chill, reserving any cooking liquid.

If using canned salmon, drain and remove any bones or skin. Flake salmon and combine with cucumber and raspberries.

In a separate container, combine the oil, vinegar and basil. Shake well. Add any cooking liquid from the salmon.

Just before serving, slice the avocados in half and remove the pits. Scoop out most of the flesh to form cups. Chop or cube the excess avocado meat and add to the salmon. Mound the salad in the avocado cups and drizzle the dressing over each. Garnish with sprigs of mint.

Makes 4 servings.

Note: If the avocados are too small to stuff, peel and cube the avocado flesh and combine with the cucumber and raspberries. Serve on lettuce leaves.

The Italian island of Sardinia is known for exotic combinations of fruit and seafood.
Green olives and raisins give the salad salty and sweet flavors.

Sardinian Sardine Salad

8 ounces shell pasta or elbow
   macaroni
1/4 cup olive oil
1 onion, thinly sliced
Juice of 1 large orange (about 1/3 cup)
1/2 cup golden raisins
1/2 cup toasted slivered almonds
1/2 cup green olives, sliced in half
2 (4 1/2-ounce cans) sardines
Lemon juice
4 tablespoons minced fresh parsley

 cooked shrimp, smoked
oysters, smoked clams

Bring a large kettle of salted water to a boil. Add the pasta and cook according to package directions until tender. Drain and set aside in a large mixing bowl.

While the pasta is cooking, heat the oil in a large skillet. Cook the onion slowly until golden brown, about 10 minutes. Add the orange juice and raisins and bring to a boil. Pour this mixture over the pasta and toss well. Add the slivered almonds, olives, parsley and sardines, including the oil in the can. Toss well, breaking up the sardines. If desired, season with lemon juice and freshly ground black pepper.

Serve at room temperature.

Makes 6 servings.

An updated classic with a mild, pink sauce.

Seafood Louis

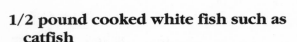

1/2 pound cooked white fish such as catfish
1/2 pound steamed, shelled shrimp
Lettuce
2 tablespoons sweet pickle relish
2 hard-boiled eggs, peeled and sliced into rounds
1 large ripe tomato, cut into 8 wedges
4 black olives (for garnish)

Dressing:
1/2 cup mayonnaise
3 tablespoons chili sauce
2 tablespoons sour cream
1 teaspoon Worcestershire sauce
1 tablespoon lemon juice
1 green onion, finely chopped
1/8 teaspoon white pepper

 cod, orange roughy, mahi mahi, butterfish

 Have the shrimp steamed for you at the store. They'll be cool and ready to shell by the time you get home.

Cut the fish into bite-sized pieces or flake with a fork.

Arrange the lettuce on plates and top with fish and shrimp. Sprinkle sweet pickle relish over the fish and arrange the eggs and tomatoes around the rim. Garnish each plate with an olive.

Combine all the ingredients for the dressing in a small bowl. Stir to combine well. Allow each diner to drizzle the dressing over the salad.

Makes 4 servings.

My good friend, Molly Losey, said her mother, Eleanor Friedman of Boca Raton, made a salad like this one when she was a child. Molly loved it so much, she would nibble on it straight from the refrigerator.

Boca Raton Seafood Salad

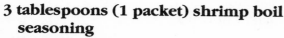

3 tablespoons (1 packet) shrimp boil seasoning
1 quart water
1 pound shrimp
1 lobster tail
5 squid, cleaned
1/4 pound cooked mussels (optional)
4 tablespoons minced fresh parsley
Garlic Tarragon Vinaigrette (recipe follows)

 Have all the seafood steamed for you at the store so you can make the salad when you get home.

Bring the shrimp seasoning and water to a boil. Boil for a few minutes until the water is colored. Reduce heat to a gentle simmer. Add the shrimp and simmer for 3 to 4 minutes, until each is gently curled. Remove shrimp with a slotted spoon. Shrimp will continue to cook after being removed from heat, so do not overcook at this point. Spread out on a baking sheet to cool.

Drop the lobster tail in the simmering water. Cook for 6 to 8 minutes, until the shell is bright red. Remove with a slotted spoon and allow to cool.

Slice the squid crosswise into rings. Cook the squid in the broth for 1 to 2 minutes, until opaque. Remove from heat and allow to cool.

Peel the shrimp and cut into 1/2-inch pieces. Use a pair of scissors to cut the lobster tail down the underside. Remove the meat and discard the shell. Cut in half lengthwise and slice the meat into small pieces.

Remove the cooked mussels from the shells and discard the shells.

Combine the seafood in a ceramic dish. Pour the dressing over all and allow to marinate overnight.

Serve chilled on lettuce leaves with lemon wedges.

Makes 8 appetizer portions.

Notes: If you wish to stretch this salad to feed more people, add about a cup each of finely chopped celery, green or red bell pepper and peeled, seeded cucumber. Frozen cooked mussel meat is available in seafood markets.

Garlic Tarragon Vinaigrette

1 clove garlic, peeled
2 tablespoons tarragon or other herb-
    flavored vinegar
3 tablespoons cider vinegar
1/2 cup canola or peanut oil
1 tablespoon whole-grain or Dijon-
    style mustard
1/4 teaspoon sugar
1/2 teaspoon mixed salad herbs
1/2 teaspoon tarragon leaves
1/4 teaspoon salt
1/4 teaspoon black pepper

Combine all the ingredients in a food processor or blender. Process until fully blended. Store any leftover dressing in the refrigerator.

Makes 3/4 cup.

Note: Wash cutting boards, hands and knives with hot soapy water after cutting up raw fish or shellfish. Bacteria from the raw seafood can contaminate what has already been cooked.

Imitation crab meat, also called by its Japanese name, surimi, has a sweet flavor very similar to crab. The chunky, flaked style works best in this recipe.

Dilled Crab and Pasta Salad

8 ounces penne or rigatoni pasta
3 tablespoons olive oil
3 tablespoons lemon juice
1 teaspoon honey
4 tablespoons fresh chopped dill or 1
   teaspoon dried dill
1/2 teaspoon salt
2 tablespoons low-fat mayonnaise
12 ounces imitation crab meat (surimi)
1 medium cucumber, peeled, seeded
   and diced (about 1 cup)
Lettuce leaves

 crab meat, shrimp, scallops

Cook the pasta in boiling, salted water according to package instructions until it's tender but not mushy. While it's cooking, combine the olive oil, lemon juice, honey, salt and mayonnaise in a jar with a tight-fitting lid. Shake well to combine. Drain pasta but do not rinse.

Pour the dressing over the warm pasta and toss to coat every noodle. Add the chopped dill, imitation crab meat and cucumber. Serve on a bed of lettuce leaves.

Makes 4 servings.

Notes: The pasta absorbs the flavor best if you pour the dressing over while hot. The dressing tastes tart at first, but gradually mellows as the salad cools. If you have leftovers, dress the salad again to perk up the flavor. This is good with a handful of crumbled feta cheese added.

A light salad with a thin, flavorful dressing.

Scallop Salad
with Creamy Cucumber Dressing

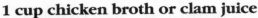

1 cup chicken broth or clam juice
**3 tablespoons lemon or lime juice,
   divided**
1 pound bay scallops
**1 small cucumber, peeled, seeded and
   chopped**
1/8 teaspoon white pepper
2 tablespoons mayonnaise
**1/4 cup sour cream or sour half and
   half**
1 tablespoon Dijon-style mustard
**1 teaspoon dried dill or 2 tablespoons
   fresh dill**
Dash hot pepper sauce
1 cup diced celery
**1 cup frozen green peas, thawed and
   drained**

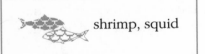

shrimp, squid

In a microwave-safe dish combine the chicken broth or clam juice and 2 tablespoons of the lemon or lime juice. Heat on high (100 percent power) until bubbling. Add the scallops and cover. Cook for 1 minute on medium (50 percent power). Stir scallops and cook for 1 to 2 minutes longer on medium (50 percent) power.

Remove the scallops from the microwave oven and allow them to cool in the broth. Drain and chill. (If desired, save broth to use in another recipe for soup or chowder.)

In a food processor or blender, combine the remaining 1 tablespoon lime or lemon juice, white pepper, mayonnaise, sour cream, mustard, dill and hot pepper sauce. Puree and add the cucumber. Chop the cucumber briefly to make a slightly chunky dressing.

Pour the dressing over the scallops and toss with the celery and green peas. For a colorful presentation, serve in halved tomatoes or in cups made from the leaves of red cabbage.

Makes 6 to 8 servings.

Bacon, Catfish and Blue Cheese Salad

2 catfish fillets, cut into 1-inch cubes
1 yellow or red pepper, roasted, peeled and sliced
1 small red onion, sliced
1 tablespoon chopped fresh dill or 1/2 teaspoon dried
1/4 cup extra virgin olive oil
1/4 cup balsamic or red wine vinegar
1 head Boston lettuce
2 cups spinach, romaine or arugula leaves
4 strips lean bacon, cooked and crumbled
3 ounces blue cheese, crumbled
Salt and pepper to taste

To prepare catfish, place fillets in skillet and add enough salted water to cover. Simmer 5-7 minutes or until fish flakes easily. Drain and cool. Cut into cubes.

In large bowl, combine catfish cubes, yellow pepper strips, red onion rings, dill, oil and vinegar. Cover and marinate 1 hour. Just before serving, arrange on lettuce leaves or arugula. Sprinkle with bacon and blue cheese.
Add salt and pepper to taste.

Makes 4 servings.

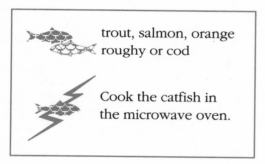

trout, salmon, orange roughy or cod

Cook the catfish in the microwave oven.

SOUPS

This Florida-style favorite has a beautiful coral-colored broth and a fine flavor. A food processor makes quick work of the chopping and grinding. Chop each ingredient separately to keep from pulverizing them.

Conch Chowder

2 slices bacon, cut into 1-inch pieces
1 medium onion, chopped
2 to 3 cloves garlic, chopped or
    crushed through a press
2 stalks celery, chopped
1 large carrot, chopped
1 small jalapeno pepper, seeded,
    cored and chopped
1 (14 1/2-ounce) can stewed tomatoes
2 tablespoons tomato paste
2 bay leaves
1 heaping teaspoon thyme
1/2 teaspoon black pepper
1/2 teaspoon salt
1 (8-ounce) bottle clam juice
6 cups water
1 pound conch, ground
2 medium red-skinned potatoes, diced
1/2 cup cream sherry
2 tablespoons flour
2 tablespoons water
2 ice cubes

 alligator, abalone, squid

Fry the bacon in a large kettle until crisp. Pour off most of the fat.

Fry the onion, garlic, celery, carrot and jalapeno pepper in the remaining bacon fat. Cook 3 to 4 minutes, until vegetables are tender. Add the tomatoes, including the juice, the tomato paste, bay leaves, thyme and salt and pepper. Stir in the clam juice, water, conch and potatoes. Bring mixture to a boil, then reduce heat to a simmer. Simmer uncovered for 40 to 45 minutes.

In a jar with a tight fitting lid, combine the flour, water and ice cubes. Shake the jar vigorously and pour the flour and water paste into the chowder. Add the sherry. Stir and increase the heat until the soup boils. Allow mixture to boil gently, stirring frequently until the broth thickens slightly.

Taste for seasoning and add more sherry if desired.

Makes 10 servings.

Notes: Conch is a mollusk encased in a beautiful spiral shell with a pink interior. The meat is extremely sweet but tough. Grinding and simmering makes it tender. Frozen conch is available in some seafood markets.

You may substitute a small green bell pepper for the jalapeno pepper.

Vatapa (Vaa-taa-PAH) is a Brazilian seafood and coconut stew. This simplified version is faster to make than the African-inspired original. It's rich and delicious.

Vatapa

3 tablespoons canola oil
1 large onion, diced (about 1 1/2 cups)
2 cloves garlic, crushed through a
   press
2 large tomatoes, seeded and chopped
1/4 teaspoon crushed hot red pepper
   or 1 Scotch bonnet pepper, finely
   minced
1 teaspoon finely chopped fresh
   ginger
2 tablespoons chopped fresh cilantro
1 (16-ounce) can coconut milk, plus 1
   can water
1/2 cup roasted, salted cashews
1 cup grated unsweetened coconut
2 to 3 tablespoons freshly squeezed
   lemon or lime juice
1 pound shrimp, shelled and deveined
2 pounds medium-firm fish, cut into
   cubes

 mackerel, kingfish, sea bass,
mahi mahi, kingklip

In a large skillet, heat the oil over medium heat. Add the onion and saute for 3 to 4 minutes until soft. Add the garlic, tomatoes, red pepper and ginger. Stir and saute for 2 to 4 minutes longer. Add the cilantro, coconut milk and water, cashews and coconut. Reduce heat to a simmer and cook for 5 to 7 minutes longer, until sauce thickens.

Remove from heat and transfer sauce to a blender or food processor. Puree in batches if necessary, adding a little water if sauce is too thick. Return sauce to skillet.

(Dish may be prepared in advance to this point. The cooled sauce can be refrigerated for up to 4 days before adding the shrimp and fish.)

Heat the sauce to a simmer. Stir in the lemon or lime juice, shrimp and cubes of fish. Cook, stirring occasionally, for 5 to 6 minutes. The shrimp should be pink and curled. Taste for salt.

Serve hot over rice.

Makes 8 servings.

Notes: Coconut milk is available in Caribbean, Latin and Oriental markets. Don't confuse it with coconut cream, which is heavily sweetened and used to make cocktails.

Unsweetened coconut is available in the frozen foods section of many supermarkets. You can also make your own by grating the meat of a fresh coconut.

Meaty Fish and Fennel Stew

3/4 pound monkfish
3/4 pound shark
1 tablespoon olive oil
1 bunch green onions, chopped
  (about 1 1/2 cups)
1 clove garlic, crushed through a press
1/2 teaspoon fennel seeds
3/4 teaspoon salt
1 teaspoon oregano
1/2 cup white wine
2 cups water
2 (14 1/2-ounce) cans clear chicken
  broth
1 (15-ounce) can tomato sauce
10 tiny red-skinned potatoes, cut in
  half
1 (10-ounce) box frozen artichoke
  hearts, thawed
1 (10-ounce) box frozen corn

 mussels, marlin, skate

Cut the shark and monkfish into 1-inch cubes. Refrigerate.

In a large kettle, cook the green onions over medium heat in the olive oil until soft, about 3 minutes. Add the garlic, fennel seeds, oregano and salt and cook about 1 to 2 minutes longer. Add the white wine, water, chicken broth, tomato sauce and potatoes and bring to a boil. Simmer for 15 to 20 minutes. Add the shark and monkfish. When the liquid returns to a boil, reduce the heat to a simmer and cook for 5 minutes. Add the artichokes and corn. Allow the mixture to return to a simmer and cook for 5 to 6 minutes longer.

Serve in shallow soup bowl with crusty bread for dipping or Buttered Croutons (recipe page 202).

Makes 12 servings.

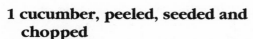 *This fresh, summery soup tastes even better the second day— and it freezes beautifully.*

Seafood Gazpacho

1 cucumber, peeled, seeded and chopped

2 large tomatoes, seeded and chopped

1 clove garlic, peeled

1 small onion, peeled and coarsely chopped (about 1/2 cup)

1 red bell pepper, seeded and chopped

1 green bell pepper, seeded and chopped

1/4 cup chopped fresh cilantro

1/2 teaspoon salt

1/4 teaspoon freshly ground black pepper

3 cups Bloody Mary mix

1/2 cup dry sherry or white wine

1 tablespoon Worcestershire sauce

2 tablespoons lemon juice

1 tablespoon olive oil

1 pound steamed small shrimp, shelled

12 ounces lump crab meat, picked over to remove pieces of shell and cartilage

In a blender or food processor, combine the cucumber, tomatoes, garlic, onion, red and green bell peppers and cilantro. Process until mixture is in coarse chunks.

Transfer to a large serving bowl and stir in salt and pepper. Pour Bloody Mary mix, sherry or white wine, Worcestershire sauce, lemon juice and olive oil over the vegetables. Stir. Chill for at least 15 minutes to allow flavors to blend.

Just before serving, stir in shrimp and crabmeat. Serve chilled. Garnish each serving of soup with a dollop of sour cream, if desired.

Makes 6 to 8 servings.

Notes: For a zestier soup, use extra-spicy Bloody Mary mix.

 scallops, squid, clams

This soup has a delicate flavor and a beautiful, pale lemon color.

Curried Cream of Scallop Soup

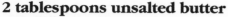

2 tablespoons unsalted butter
1 tablespoon olive oil
1 medium onion, chopped (about
  1 1/4 cups)
2 cloves garlic, crushed through a
  press
1 tablespoon curry powder
1/2 teaspoon cumin
1/4 teaspoon cardamom
2 teaspoons sugar
3 tablespoons flour
1 1/4 teaspoons salt
3 cups water
2 tablespoons lemon juice
2 pounds bay scallops or sea scallops
2 cups milk
Buttered Croutons (recipe page 202)

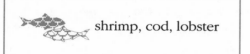
shrimp, cod, lobster

In a kettle, melt the butter and add the olive oil. Saute the onion and garlic over medium-high heat for 1 to 2 minutes, stirring often. In a small dish, combine the curry powder, cumin, cardamom, flour, sugar and salt. Pour the spice mixture into the onions, stirring with a wire whisk to blend. Cook for 1 minute, until the mixture is fragrant.

Pour in about 1 cup of the water, whisking constantly to blend the flour into the liquid. Add remaining water and bring mixture to a boil. Sauce will thicken slightly when it boils. Add the lemon juice, reduce heat and simmer gently for 5 minutes.

Stir in the scallops and milk. Cook over low heat for 10 minutes but don't let the soup come to a boil. Serve in shallow soup bowls, sprinkled with Buttered Croutons.

Makes 8 servings.

Notes: The curry in this soup is delicate so the flavor of the scallops isn't obliterated. If you like foods spicier, or if substituting fish or shellfish with a more pronounced flavor, add more curry powder to taste.

A hearty, chunky soup tailor-made for a cool fall day.

Saffron Chowder

3/4 pound cod fillets
3/4 pound medium-firm fish fillets
1 tablespoon olive oil
1 small onion, chopped (about 1 cup)
2 stalks celery, chopped (about 1 cup)
2 large cloves garlic, crushed through a press
1 red or yellow pepper, diced (about 1 cup)
1 teaspoon turmeric
1/2 teaspoon saffron threads or 1/4 teaspoon powdered saffron
1 cup dry white wine
8 ounces bottled clam juice
4 cups water
2 bay leaves
1/2 teaspoon thyme leaves
1/8 teaspoon crushed red pepper
1/2 teaspoon salt or to taste
1/2 cup small shell pasta, uncooked
2 tablespoons lemon juice
4 tablespoons chopped fresh parsley

Cut the fish into 1-inch cubes. Refrigerate.

In a large kettle, heat the oil and saute the onion, celery, garlic and bell pepper for 5 minutes. Add the turmeric and saffron and cook for 2 minutes longer, until fragrant.

Stir in the white wine, clam juice and water. Add the bay leaves, thyme, crushed red pepper and salt and bring the mixture to a boil. Reduce heat and simmer for 10 minutes.

Add the shell pasta and cook for 3 minutes, until pasta is almost tender. Add fish and simmer gently for 10 minutes.

Remove bay leaves and stir in lemon juice. Garnish with parsley. Serve hot with garlic bread or a salad.

Makes 6 servings.

tuna, amberjack, bluefish, grouper, Pacific rockfish, mahi mahi

This is a seafood lover's dream with big chunks of fish simmering in a velvety broth. The intense flavor comes from using pureed tomatoes, celery and carrots to thicken the broth instead of cream.

Florida Red Chowder

2 pounds fish fillets
1 tablespoon olive oil
1 large onion, sliced
2 carrots, chopped
2 stalks celery, chopped
3 cloves garlic, peeled
1 (8-ounce) bottle clam juice
1 cup white wine or chicken broth
1 cup water
6 to 8 small-to-medium red potatoes, peeled and chopped (about 3 1/2 cups)
1 (28-ounce) can stewed, peeled tomatoes including juice
2 tablespoons tomato paste
1 1/4 teaspoon dried thyme
1 tablespoon Worcestershire sauce
1/4 teaspoon salt
2 teaspoons hot sauce or to taste
8 tablespoons Parmesan cheese for garnish (optional)

red snapper, pompano, mahi mahi, cod, Pacific rockfish

Cut fish into chunks, removing any skin or bones. Refrigerate.

Heat the oil in a large kettle over medium heat. Add the onion, carrots, celery and garlic. Saute, stirring occasionally, until onions are soft and transparent. Add the potatoes, tomatoes, tomato paste, thyme, Worcestershire sauce, salt, clam juice, wine or broth and water. Bring to a boil, then reduce heat to a simmer. Simmer covered for 30 to 35 minutes.

Using a slotted spoon, strain vegetables out of the broth. Puree the vegetables until smooth in a food mill, blender or food processor. Return the pureed mixture to the kettle and stir to combine. Taste for seasoning.

Heat the mixture to a simmer over low heat. Add the fish and cook, stirring occasionally to prevent sticking, for 10 to 12 minutes longer.

Garnish each portion with optional Parmesan cheese and serve warm.

Makes 8 servings.

Notes: The pureed broth can be made in advance and refrigerated for up to two days before adding the fish. If desired, the broth can be frozen up to three months before thawing and adding the fish. If desired, use a mixture of fish and shellfish in this soup.

With a wedge of bread and a green salad, you can make a full meal of this filling soup.

Potato and Salmon Chowder

1 tablespoon olive oil
1 leek, washed and sliced (about 1 1/2 cups)
1 red bell pepper, diced (about 1 1/2 cups)
2 large baking potatoes, peeled and diced into 1/4-inch pieces
3 cups chicken broth
2 teaspoons dried thyme
2 bay leaves
1/2 teaspoon cayenne pepper or to taste
1 cup low-fat milk
3/4 pound salmon, skin and bones removed, cut in 1/2-inch pieces
1/2 teaspoon salt
1/4 cup chopped fresh parsley

In a large, microwave-safe dish, combine the olive oil, leeks and bell pepper. Cook on high (100 percent) power for 3 minutes.

Stir in potatoes, broth, thyme, bay leaves and cayenne and cook on medium-high (70 percent) power for 12 minutes. Rotate dish every 3 minutes. Stir and cook on medium-high (70 percent) power for 6 minutes longer, until potatoes are tender. Discard bay leaves.

Use a slotted spoon to transfer 4 cups of the potatoes to a food processor or blender. Add the milk and puree until smooth.

Return the potato mixture to the dish and add the salmon and salt. Cook on high (100 percent) power for 3 to 4 minutes. Sprinkle with parsley and allow to stand 3 minutes before serving.

Makes 6 servings.

During cold weather, nothing tastes better than creamy, steamy chowder. This one is ready in a flash.

20-Minute Clam Chowder

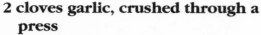

2 cloves garlic, crushed through a press
1 small onion, chopped
2 tablespoons olive oil
2 (10 1/2-ounce) cans chicken broth
1 (6 1/2-ounce) can clams, drained with liquid reserved
2 (10 3/4-ounce) cans cream of potato soup, undiluted
1 large baking potato, peeled and cut into 1/2-inch pieces
1/4 teaspoon pepper
1/2 cup milk or more as necessary

In a large kettle on medium-high heat cook the garlic and onion in the olive oil for 4 to 5 minutes, until tender. Add broth, reserved juice from the can of clams, potato soup and diced potato. Stir in pepper and bring to a simmer.

Cook 20 minutes. Add milk and drained clams. If mixture is too thick, add extra milk. Heat through but don't allow the soup to boil.

Makes 6 servings.

Notes: There is some variation between cans of potato soup. Some cans are very thick, some cans are thin. Adjust the thickness of the chowder by adding more or less milk.

A fast and easy version of a soup popular in Thai restaurants. The color is slightly gray but the flavor is spectacular.

Thai Lime and Shrimp Soup

2 tablespoons minced ginger
1/4 teaspoon crushed red pepper
4 cups chicken broth, canned or
   homemade
1 lime peel, green rind only, sliced
   into threads
1/2 pound medium shrimp, peeled
   and deveined
4 large mushrooms, sliced
1 cup canned unsweetened coconut
   milk
1 teaspoon soy sauce
3 green onions, finely chopped
2 tablespoons fresh lime juice

Combine 1 cup of the chicken broth and the ginger, red pepper and lime peel in a large kettle or saucepan. Bring to a high boil and cook for 10 minutes until the liquid has reduced slightly. Add the remaining chicken broth, lower the heat to a simmer and cook for 20 minutes.

Just before serving, add the shrimp, coconut milk, soy sauce, mushrooms, green onions and lime juice. Simmer until shrimp are pink and curled, about 3 to 4 minutes. Allow soup to stand for a few moments. Stir to prevent soup from separating.

Makes 4 to 6 servings.

Note: Coconut milk is available in Oriental, Latin American and Indian markets. Do not use the sweetened coconut cream used to make cocktails.

A thick, hearty main-course soup. Vary the vegetables according to the season.

Italian Garden Chowder

2 pounds fish fillets
1 (28-ounce) can crushed tomatoes
1 (8-ounce) bottle clam juice
1 cup white wine
1 onion, chopped (about 1 cup)
2 cloves garlic, crushed through a
   press
1 teaspoon rosemary leaves
1 teaspoon oregano
1/4 teaspoon thyme
1/2 teaspoon salt
1/4 teaspoon sugar
1 stalk celery, chopped
1 carrot, peeled and chopped
6 small red-skinned potatoes, cut in
   half
3 small zucchini, cut into 1-inch
   pieces (about 2 1/2 cups)
1 (15-ounce) can garbanzo beans,
   drained

mahi mahi, cod, tuna,
mackerel, monkfish

Cut the fish into cubes. Refrigerate.

In a large kettle, combine the tomatoes, clam juice, wine, onion, garlic, herbs, salt, sugar, celery and carrot. Bring to a boil and simmer for 15 to 20 minutes. Add the potatoes and cook for 10 minutes longer. Add the zucchini, garbanzo beans and fish. Simmer soup gently for 5 to 7 minutes longer.

Serve in soup plates with Parmesan cheese sprinkled on top. Have Italian bread on hand for dipping.

Makes 6 servings.

This is an easy soup to make in two stages. Prepare the broth one day and add the fish and shrimp the next.

Catfish and Shrimp Soup

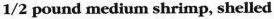

1/2 pound medium shrimp, shelled
2 catfish fillets, cut into 1-inch cubes
2 tablespoons olive oil
1 large yellow onion, chopped (about 2 cups)
2 cloves garlic, crushed through a press
1 (28-ounce) can crushed tomatoes
3 tablespoons tomato paste
1 bay leaf
4 cups water
1 cup dry white wine
1 (8-ounce) bottle clam juice
1/2 teaspoon salt
1/4 teaspoon pepper
Parsley and lemon slices for garnish

Cut catfish into cubes. Set catfish and shrimp aside in the refrigerator.

In large soup pot, heat oil. Saute onion and garlic until onions are transparent, about 5 minutes. Add tomatoes, tomato paste and bay leaf. Cover and simmer 25 minutes. Add water, wine and clam juice. Simmer uncovered 30 minutes. (If making the soup in two stages, cool the broth and refrigerate until ready to cook. Heat the broth to boiling before adding the fish and shellfish.)

Add shrimp, catfish, salt and pepper. Cook 10 minutes, or until catfish flakes easily. Remove bay leaf. Garnish each serving with chopped parsley and lemon slices.

Makes 8 servings.

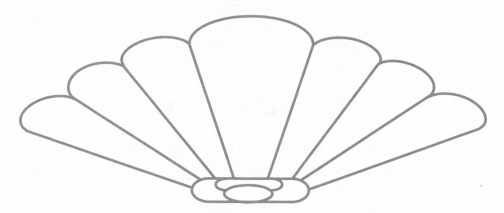

ON THE GRILL

Grilling tips

Use a hinged wire grill basket for cooking whole fish such as snapper, trout or salmon. Grill baskets are usually available where grilling accessories are sold.

Use a grilling basket for fillets of tender fish such as catfish, snapper, perch or flounder.

Skewer small shellfish such as shrimp or scallops or cook them in a grill basket.

Fillets of firm fish, such as tuna, salmon, shark or swordfish can be cooked directly on the grill.

Grill over medium to medium-low heat.

Turn fish only once.

If using a marinade, allow fish to soak up flavor for at least 30 minutes.

Do not serve cooked fish or seafood in the marinade unless the liquid has been boiled for at least 5 minutes.

Shellfish in the shell, such as oysters, mussels and clams can be cooked directly on the hottest part of the grill. They're done when the shell opens. Discard those that don't open after about 5 minutes.

To get a diamond pattern on grilled fish:

Start with the grill heated to medium-high.

Brush both sides of the fish lightly with olive oil or canola oil.

Cook without turning on first side for 2 to 3 minutes.

Rotate fish 45-degress on the grill or give it one-quarter turn and cook for 2 to 3 minutes longer.

Flip fish and cook the same way on the other side.

If you're not sure grilled fish is done, you can finish cooking it in a microwave oven:

Cook fish or seafood for half the required time on a barbecue grill. This gives the fish the attractive grill marks and some grilled flavor.

Transfer the fish to a microwave-safe baking dish and cook 1 to 2 minutes to finish cooking the fish. Press or flake with a fork to test for doneness.

Remember, fish continues to cook after it is removed from the microwave oven so allow 1 to 2 minutes standing time before you cook it any longer.

The secret to this exquisite mixed feast is putting items on the grill at different intervals so the long-cooking vegetables and quick-cooking fish are ready to eat all at one time. A good bottle of Napa Valley Lakespring chardonnay is a fine match to the meal.

Grilled Tuna and Vegetables with Orange Vinaigrette

2 pounds fresh tuna steaks, about 1-inch thick
12 small red-skinned potatoes, washed
2 red or yellow bell peppers, pierced once with a knife
3 zucchini, ends trimmed
2 heads radicchio (red chicory)
Orange Vinaigrette (recipe follows)

 swordfish, shark, mahi mahi, snapper

Cut the tuna into 6 even pieces. Set aside.

Heat a grill until the coals are medium hot. Pierce the peppers with a knife and place them on the hottest part of the grill. The skin should blister and char slightly after 12 minutes. Place in a sturdy plastic bag or food storage container with an airtight lid. Allow to steam and cool. When cool enough to handle, peel away and discard the skin.

If desired, thread all the potatoes on metal skewer. Place them over the hottest part of the fire. Cook for 25 to 30 minutes, turning occasionally and basting with the Orange Vinaigrette.

Add the zucchini and cook until the squash are slightly blackened but tender. Baste occasionally with Orange Vinaigrette. Zucchini will require about 8 to 10 minutes total cooking time.

Add the tuna steaks and cook for 6 minutes per side. Baste occasionally with Orange Vinaigrette. Slice the radicchio in half lengthwise and add to the grill. Baste with the vinaigrette. Cook for 4 to 5 minutes, until the leaves are wilted and slightly charred. Remove all vegetables and fish from the grill. Keep warm.

Transfer remaining Orange Vinaigrette to a microwave-safe container. Cook on high (100 percent) power for 2 minutes, stirring occasionally until the mixture boils. Drizzle over hot vegetables and fish and serve.

Makes 6 servings.

Orange Vinaigrette

2 tablespoons olive oil
1 teaspoon chopped fresh ginger
1 tablespoon low-sodium soy sauce
1 teaspoon freshly grated orange rind
1 cup freshly squeezed orange juice
2 tablespoons vinegar, such as raspberry, balsamic or white wine
Pinch cayenne pepper
1 teaspoon dry mustard

Combine all the ingredients. Blend well. Transfer to a container with an airtight lid.

Dressing can be made up to one week in advance.

Makes 1 1/4 cups.

The 1992 Summer Olympics in Barcelona, Spain, turned the world's culinary spotlight on Spanish cuisine.

Spanish-Style Grilled Fish with Olive and Pimento Relish

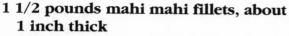

1 1/2 pounds mahi mahi fillets, about
   1 inch thick
2 tablespoons olive oil, divided
1/4 teaspoon white pepper
1/4 teaspoon salt
1/2 cup green olives with pimentos
1 clove garlic, crushed through a press
1 medium tomato, seeded and
   chopped
1 tablespoon sherry vinegar
1/2 teaspoon thyme leaves

 sea bass, wolffish, sword-fish, tuna, snapper with skin on

Pat the fish dry and brush both sides with 1 teaspoon olive oil. Sprinkle the salt over both sides. Heat a grill to medium-hot. Grill the fish for 6 minutes on the first side and 5 minutes on the second side. Transfer to a warm platter.

While the fish is grilling, chop the tomato and olives into pea-sized pieces. Add the pepper, garlic, sherry vinegar, thyme and remaining 1 tablespoon olive oil. Stir to blend. Serve on top of the fish.

Makes 4 servings.

Note: If you prefer a warm sauce, prepare the olive mixture as described. Place in a microwave-safe dish and cook on high (100 percent) power for 1 to 2 minutes.

My sister-in-law, Diane, loves all things Italian, including the simple flavors of rustic Italian cooking. She uses Italian proscuitto in this recipe; I like the salty pastrami.

Basil Scallops in Pastrami

12 large sea scallops
6 paper-thin slices lean pastrami
12 large basil leaves
2 tablespoons balsamic vinegar
1 tablespoon olive oil

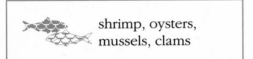
shrimp, oysters, mussels, clams

Cut the pastrami into long slices about 2 inches wide. Trim away the fat. Lay the pastrami on a work surface and place a basil leaf on one end. Top basil leaf with a scallop. Roll the pastrami around the basil leaf and scallop and tuck in any loose ends to make a tidy bundle. Thread on metal or bamboo skewers.

Mix the balsamic vinegar and the olive oil.

Grill over medium-hot heat, basting frequently with the vinegar and oil mixture, for 3 to 4 minutes per side.

Serve hot.

Makes 2 servings.

Notes: Proscuitto, a type of salted, air-dried Italian ham, also works well in this recipe. Make sure it is very thinly sliced. Country ham is a less expensive alternative. For individual appetizers, thread the scallops on toothpicks.

The easiest way to prepare this dish is have one person grill the fish while someone else sautes the mushroom topping. My husband, Peter, is the grill master in our house.

Mahi Mahi with Fancy Mushrooms

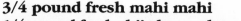

3/4 pound fresh mahi mahi
1/4 pound fresh shiitake mushrooms, stems removed and caps sliced
1/4 pound fresh oyster mushrooms, separated into individual mushrooms
3 tablespoons olive oil, divided
1 clove garlic, crushed through a press
3 tablespoons dry white wine
1 tablespoon apple juice, white grape juice or water
1/4 teaspoon salt
1/8 teaspoon white or black pepper
2 tablespoons chopped fresh basil or 1/2 teaspoon dried basil

 tuna, swordfish, shark, snapper

Brush the fish on both sides with 1 tablespoon of the olive oil. Grill fish, skin side down over medium-low heat for 8 to 10 minutes, depending on thickness.

While fish is grilling, prepare the mushrooms. Heat the remaining oil in a large, non-stick skillet. Saute the mushrooms over medium heat until they begin to wilt and turn dark brown. Add the garlic and cook, stirring, for 1 minute. Add the wine and juice or water. Cook, stirring, until the liquid boils and begins to evaporate. Stir in the salt, pepper and basil. Cook for 1 to 2 minutes longer, until the mushrooms have absorbed the liquid. Serve hot over the grilled fish.

Makes 2 servings.

Note: Shiitake and oyster mushrooms were originally imported from Japan but now they're grown in Pennsylvania, California, Washington and Vermont. Shiitake mushrooms have dark brown caps with a meaty flavor. Oyster mushrooms grow in delicate clusters of yellow-gray, fan-shaped caps with pale stems. The flavor is slightly peppery and, when cooked, reminiscent of oysters. Substitute other kinds of mushrooms such as crimini (brown field mushrooms), chanterelle (French trumpets) or enoki (tiny Japanese white mushrooms) in this recipe.

Screwdrivers are cocktails made with orange juice and vodka. This recipe uses the same ingredients to make a light, refreshing marinade for grilled fish.

Salmon Screwdrivers

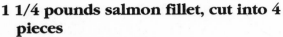

1 1/4 pounds salmon fillet, cut into 4 pieces
1/4 cup lemon vodka
1/4 cup fresh orange juice
1 tablespoon lemon juice
1/2 teaspoon sugar
2 heaping tablespoons whole-grained mustard
1/2 teaspoon dried dill or 2 tablespoons chopped fresh dill
2 oranges, peeled and sectioned

 grouper, halibut, swordfish, tuna, cod, pompano

Arrange the fish in a glass or ceramic dish. Combine the vodka, orange and lemon juice, sugar, mustard and dill. Stir well to dissolve sugar. Pour the vodka mixture over the fish. Refrigerate and allow to marinate for 1 to 3 hours. Turn the fish occasionally to coat both sides.

Heat a grill to medium-high heat. Cook the fish for 10 minutes per inch of thickness, basting every few minutes with the marinade. Fish is done when it is firm to the touch. Discard marinade.

Transfer to a platter or 4 serving plates. Garnish top with orange sections. Serve with rice or Grill-Toasted Garlic Bread. (recipe page 211)

Makes 4 servings.

Notes: A miniature bottle of lemon vodka is a few ounces shy of 1/4 cup. That scant amount doesn't make a big difference in this recipe.

 *This is the best way to grill flaky fish — steamed inside aluminum foil packets on a barbecue grill. Use fresh herbs in spring and summer!*

Herbed Tilapia in Packets

1 1/4 pounds tilapia fillets
3 tablespoons butter, cut into 8 pieces
1/8 teaspoon freshly ground black
   pepper
1 tablespoon chopped fresh basil or
   1/2 teaspoon dried
1 tablespoon chopped fresh tarragon
   or 1/2 teaspoon dried
1 tablespoon chopped fresh marjoram
   or thyme or 1/2 teaspoon dried
1 tablespoon fresh chopped chives or
   1 teaspoon dried
4 sheets of aluminum foil about
   6 inches square

 cod, snapper, grouper, catfish, perch, sea trout, flounder

Cut the fish into uniform portions. Drop 1 piece of the butter on each sheet of aluminum foil. Place a fillet on each sheet. Combine the basil, tarragon, marjoram or thyme and chives and put some of the mixture on top of each fillet. Top with remaining butter. Pull the edges up and fold both sides together securely, twisting the ends, to make a boat so the juices can't escape.

Heat a grill to medium-high. Place the packets on the cool edges of the grill and cook without turning for 12 to 15 minutes. Serve in foil and allow each diner to open the packets at the table. Provide an extra dish for the discarded foil wrapping.

Makes 4 servings.

Note: Since the grill is already hot, it's easy to cook some small, red-skinned potatoes and a few ears of corn at the same time. The potatoes take about 20 minutes to cook. If the corn is wrapped in foil, it will cook in about 10 minutes; otherwise, it will cook in about 6 minutes.

Swordfish, tuna, kingfish and other meaty fish have flavor and texture enough to stand up to very robust toppings. Cooking the onions and garlic very slowly makes them sweet and tender. This outstanding dish deserves an outstanding wine, such as a Napa Valley Lakespring merlot.

Grilled Swordfish
with Caramelized Onions and Garlic

1 1/2 pounds swordfish, sliced 3/4-inch thick

1 large Vidalia, Walla Walla, Florida Sweet, Maui or other sweet onion

2 cloves elephant garlic or 5 cloves regular garlic, thinly sliced

3 tablespoons olive oil

2 tablespoons butter

1/2 teaspoon sugar

3 tablespoons orange juice, preferably fresh squeezed (1/2 an orange)

1/4 teaspoon salt

1/4 teaspoon pepper

 tuna, mahi mahi, sea bass, mackerel, halibut

Peel the onion and slice in half lengthwise. Slice crosswise as thinly as possible. Heat the oil and butter in heavy skillet. When the butter foams, add the onions and garlic. Reduce heat to medium-low and cook the onions slowly for 20 to 25 minutes until they're golden brown. Monitor the heat to make sure the mixture doesn't burn. When the onions are golden, sprinkle with sugar, orange juice, salt and pepper. Allow the juice to evaporate for about 1 minute.

About 10 minutes before the onions are done, heat a grill to medium-high. Brush both sides of the swordfish with olive or vegetable oil. Cook the fish for 2 minutes; rotate the fish one-quarter turn without flipping it. (This gives the fish an attractive diamond pattern from the grill.) Cook for 5 minutes longer on the same side.

Flip fish and cook for 5 minutes longer. Fish is done when it feels firm to the touch.

Serve topped with caramelized onions. Makes 4 servings.

In this recipe, the classic refers to Coke Classic. Don't try this one with Diet Coke!

Classic Grilled Shrimp

1/2 cup Coca-Cola
2 tablespoons freshly squeezed lime
   juice
1 clove garlic, crushed through a press
1 teaspoon brown sugar
30 medium shrimp

 sea scallops, cubed tuna, swordfish or shark

Shell the shrimp, leaving the tails intact if you wish. In a glass or ceramic dish, combine the Coke, lime juice, garlic and sugar. Stir to dissolve the sugar. Marinate the shrimp in the refrigerator for 1 to 2 hours.

Heat a grill to medium. Drain the shrimp and thread on bamboo skewers so all the shrimp are facing one direction.

Cook the shrimp, basting occasionally, for 4 minutes. Turn and cook on the other side for 4 minutes longer. Don't overcook.

Makes 4 servings.

Note: When using bamboo skewers, it's a good idea to soak them in cold water for about 15 minutes before spearing the shrimp or shellfish. The water will help prevent them from burning. If the fire is too hot, the skewers will burn anyway. Don't grill fish or shellfish over a flame that is too high.

Sherried Shrimp

1 pound large shrimp, shelled and
deveined
2 tablespoons Roasted Garlic Oil
   (recipe page 203)
4 tablespoons sherry vinegar

scallops, chunks of
tuna, mahi mahi or
kingfish, medallions
of lobster

Combine the Roasted Garlic Oil, sherry and shrimp in a glass dish. Refrigerate and allow to marinate for 30 minutes to 1 hour. Drain and thread from head to tail on metal skewers. Grill over medium-high heat for 4 minutes, basting frequently with the marinade. Turn and grill for 2 to 4 minutes longer, until the shrimp are pink and firm. Don't overcook.

Makes 4 to 5 servings.

Ginger-Grilled Salmon or Swordfish

1 1/3 pounds fish steaks
3 tablespoons lemon juice
2 tablespoons honey
1 tablespoon finely grated fresh
   ginger
1 tablespoon low-sodium soy sauce
1/2 teaspoon Chinese five-spice
   powder
Freshly ground black pepper to taste

tuna, butterfish, shark,
halibut

Combine the lemon juice, honey, ginger, soy sauce and five-spice powder in a shallow dish. Coat both sides of the salmon or halibut with the mixture and marinate for 30 to 35 minutes.

Drain fish and reserve marinade. Grill over medium-low heat for 6 minutes per side, basting frequently. Turn and cook for 5 to 6 minutes on the other side. Discard marinade. Do not allow flames to flare up and scorch the fish. The honey in the marinade will burn if exposed to direct flames.

Makes 4 servings.

Skewers of Scallops, Shrimp and Bacon

1/2 pound sea scallops
3/4 pound shrimp
1/4 pound bacon (about 5 strips), cut
   in thirds widthwise

 cubes of swordfish, tuna
or halibut

Wrap each scallop in a piece of bacon. Peel the shrimp and thread on metal skewers through the tail and the head portion. Alternate with the scallops. Grill over low heat, for 5 to 6 minutes. Do not allow flames to flare up and scorch the seafood. Do not overcook.

Makes 4 servings.

A regular farmers' market in one very easy dish.

Grilled Fish
with a Sauce of Summer Vegetables

2 1/2 pounds fillets or steaks, about 1 inch thick
Juice of 1/2 lemon
3 tablespoons plus 1 tablespoon olive oil
1/2 red onion, sliced into thin strips
1 clove garlic, crushed through a press
1 zucchini, thinly sliced
2 small ripe tomatoes, seeded and chopped
2 teaspoons sugar
1/4 teaspoon salt
1/4 teaspoon black pepper
2 teaspoons dried basil or 4 tablespoons fresh chopped basil
4 tablespoons raspberry or tarragon vinegar

 halibut, tuna, mahi mahi, salmon, grouper

Brush the fish fillets with 1 tablespoon olive oil. Grill for 5 minutes over medium-high coals. Turn fish and squeeze lemon juice over fillets. Cook for 5 minutes longer. Remove and keep warm.

While fish is cooking, heat remaining 3 tablespoons olive oil in a non-stick skillet. Add the red onion and saute over medium-high heat for 3 to 4 minutes, until soft. Add the garlic, zucchini and tomatoes and cook for 3 to 4 minutes longer. Sprinkle with the sugar, salt and pepper and stir in the basil. Pour the vinegar over all and bring to a boil. Stir and cook ingredients together for about 2 minutes.

Spoon vegetables over hot, grilled fish.

Makes 6 servings.

Note: Cooking times will vary according to the thickness of the fish. Remember that fish continues to cook for about 1 minute after it is removed from heat, so don't overcook it.

Mild fish with an excellent, creamy, nut-flavored topping.

Glazed Halibut with Hazelnuts

2 pounds halibut steaks
1 tablespoon olive oil
4 tablespoons fresh lime or lemon juice
6 tablespoons mayonnaise
1/2 teaspoon dried marjoram or thyme
3 tablespoons coarsely chopped, toasted hazelnuts
3 tablespoons minced fresh parsley

 mahi mahi, tuna, kingfish steaks, sea bass, snapper, grouper

Rinse the halibut steaks and pat dry with paper towels. Brush both sides with olive oil.

Combine the lime or lemon juice with the mayonnaise and marjoram. Divide sauce in half. Heat a barbecue grill to medium-high. Cook the halibut for 4 to 5 minutes on one side, brushing frequently with one-half of the mayonnaise mixture. Turn and cook for 4 to 5 minutes on the second side, basting frequently. Watch carefully for flare-ups and don't allow the baste to burn.

Fish is done when it's firm to the touch and the meat is opaque.

Transfer to plates and top with remaining half of the sauce, hazelnuts and parsley.

Makes 6 servings.

Note: Other nuts, such as pecans, walnuts or pine nuts can substitute in this recipe. Shop for hazelnuts during the holiday season and store them in the freezer.

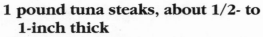

Marinating the fish makes it moist and gives it an intense flavor. Serve with a salad, a good Oregon pinot noir wine and Grill-Toasted Garlic Bread (page 211).

Tuna Teriyaki

1 pound tuna steaks, about 1/2- to 1-inch thick
1/2 cup low-sodium soy sauce
3 tablespoons lemon juice
3 tablespoons sherry or mirin
1 green onion, finely chopped
1 tablespoon finely chopped fresh ginger
1 teaspoon sugar
1 clove garlic, crushed through a press

 mahi mahi, shark, halibut, swordfish, salmon

Combine all the ingredients except tuna in a glass or ceramic baking dish. Make sure the sugar dissolves. Add the tuna and turn to coat both sides. Cover and refrigerate for 2 to 3 hours or until ready to cook.

When ready to cook, preheat grill and brush lightly with a coating of salad oil. Drain the tuna and place each piece of fish on the grill. Baste frequently and cook for 2 to 3 minutes; give each fillet a quarter-turn without flipping it. (The quarter-turn gives the fillets an attractive diamond pattern from the grill.) Cook 2 minutes longer.

Turn fillets over, baste and cook 4 minutes on the second side for medium-rare or 5 minutes for medium. Allow a few minutes longer for extremely thick pieces of fish but do not overcook.

Makes 2 to 4 servings.

Note: Mirin is sweetened sake wine.

This recipe is pure simplicity so use very fresh fish.

Grilled Whole Fish

1 (3-to-4 pound) fish, scales and gills
   removed
1 tablespoon olive oil
1 lemon, thinly sliced and seeded
Salt and freshly ground black pepper,
   to taste

 tilefish, snapper, sea bass,
bluefish, butterfish, mackerel

Wash the fish inside and out. Pat dry with paper towels. Using a sharp knife, make 2 shallow diagonal cuts on each side of the fish. Rub the outside with the olive oil, including the meat in the cuts. Squeeze a few slices of the lemon in the cavity, season lightly with salt and pepper and overlap remaining lemon slices in the cavity.

Secure the fish inside a hinged, wire grill basket. Cook over medium heat for 8 minutes. Turn and cook about 8 to 12 minutes longer, depending on thickness of fish. The meat in the slashes will be opaque and firm when done.

To serve the fish, lift off the skin starting from the diagonal cuts. Make a shallow incision down center of fish from head to tail. Gently lift the part of the fillet that is closest to the backbone away from the backbone and the ribs. Most of the ribs should stay attached to the backbone. Remove the part of the fillet that is closest to the belly. Gently remove any meat that clings to the ribs and backbone. Pick up the tail and pull the backbone and ribs away from the fillet underneath. The head, if on, should stay attached to the backbone.

Remove lemon slices before serving.

Makes 4 to 6 servings depending on size of fish.

The flavor of squid, called calamari by Italian cooks, is exquisite with garlicky pesto sauce. Commercial pesto sauce is available in the refrigerated foods section of many grocery stores.

Grilled Squid with Pesto Stuffing

8 medium whole squid, about 4 inches long
1 cup soft, fresh bread crumbs
1/2 cup pesto sauce, commercial or homemade
2 to 3 tablespoons water
1/2 teaspoon sugar
2 tablespoons olive oil (for basting)
Lemon wedges (for garnish)

 Prepare the stuffing up to 2 days in advance and store in the refrigerator. Stuff the squid up to 4 hours before cooking.

Have the squid cleaned at the market, leaving the sacs intact.

If you clean the squid, lay it down on a work surface and use a small sharp knife to cut off the tentacles just below the eyes. Cut out the hard beak in the center and discard. Reserve the tentacles. Pull the viscera out of the body. It comes out easily and is very clean. Remove and discard the thin, transparent quill. Peel off the skin and discard. Rinse the squid under running water.

Chop the tentacles and combine them in a bowl with the bread crumbs, pesto, sugar and as much water as necessary to moisten the stuffing. Stir well to combine. The mixture should be damp enough to clump together.

Stuff the filling in the cavities of the squid. Do not overstuff or stuff all the way to the opening of the sac. Secure the opening with a toothpick or a metal trussing skewer. Brush the outside generously with olive oil.

Grill over medium-high for 6 to 8 minutes, turning and basting frequently. Do not overcook or squid will become tough.

Makes 4 servings.

Nothing is better for a fast summer meal than quickly grilled fish. The steaks should be about 1-inch thick for best results.

Garlicky Grilled Tuna

1 to 1 1/2 pounds tuna steaks
2 to 3 cloves garlic, crushed through a
  press
1/4 cup olive oil
2 tablespoons chopped fresh basil or
  1 teaspoon dried basil
2 tablespoons red wine vinegar

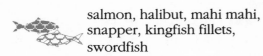
salmon, halibut, mahi mahi, snapper, kingfish fillets, swordfish

Combine the garlic, olive oil, herbs and vinegar in a shallow dish. Stir to combine. Add the fish steaks and turn to coat evenly. Cover and refrigerate at least 30 minutes or up to several hours. (If desired, marinate the fish in the morning and cook it in the evening.)

Heat a barbecue grill to medium high. Place the steaks on the grill and cook for 6 minutes on the first side, basting frequently with the marinade. Turn fish and cook for 5 to 6 minutes longer. Don't baste the fish after you have turned.

Do not overcook the fish or it will be dry.

Makes 4 servings.

 *For a light, healthful summer dinner, nothing beats these skewers of mixed grilled fish and shellfish.*

Seafood Brochettes

3 tablespoons fresh lemon juice
1 tablespoon olive oil
1 to 2 cloves garlic, crushed through a
   press
1/4 teaspoon freshly ground black
   pepper
2 tablespoons fresh herbs, such as
   basil, oregano or thyme
4 jumbo shrimp, peeled and deveined
1/2 pound fresh mahi mahi
4 sea scallops
1/2 pound fresh tuna fillet

 halibut, shark, squid,
salmon, swordfish

Combine the lemon juice, olive oil, pepper and herbs in a glass dish. Stir with a fork to blend.

Combine the shrimp and scallops in the marinade, turning to coat completely. Cut the mahi mahi and tuna into 1 1/2-inch cubes and add to the marinade. Marinate at least 20 minutes, turning frequently. (Seafood can be marinated up to a day in advance.) Divide the seafood evenly among 4 metal skewers. Grill over medium-low heat for about 10 minutes, basting often with the marinade. Fish is done when it is firm to the touch and opaque. Do not overcook. Discard marinade. Serve immediately with a green vegetable or a salad and Fresh Corn Pancakes (recipe page 201).

Makes 4 servings.

Note: For the best flavor use fresh herbs in this recipe. However, if fresh is not available, substitute 1/2 teaspoon of dried herb blend.

The simplest version of lobster, with all the flavor and none of the messy cracking. Use 6- to 8-ounce Maine lobster tails.

Grilled Lobster Tail

4 lobster tails
3 tablespoons olive oil
2 tablespoons lemon juice
1/2 teaspoon garlic powder
1/2 teaspoon onion powder
1/2 teaspoon paprika

Using a large sharp or serrated knife, slice each lobster tail in half lengthwise. With a paring knife, cut the membranes along the shell to make the lobster easier to remove.

Heat a grill to medium-hot. Stir together the olive oil, lemon juice, garlic and onion powders and paprika. Generously brush the lobster with the oil mixture and place shell-side down on the grill. Cook for 10 to 12 minutes without turning until meat is snow-white and tails are curved. Brush frequently with olive oil mixture.

Makes 4 to 8 servings.

Note: Lobster tails can cook unevenly because they are thick at the top and thin at the tip. Watch closely. If the meat closest to the fin is white and the shell is bright red, but the meat in the center isn't done, place each tail individually in a microwave oven and cook on high (100 percent) power for 30 to 60 seconds. This final "zapping" should be enough to finish cooking the lobster without making it dry.

Indonesian-style peanut sauces are an exotic combination of peanut butter (or ground peanuts), soy sauce, sugar and chili. It's excellent on shrimp, monkfish or halibut. This version is lighter and faster than most.

Shrimp Satay
with Indonesian Peanut Sauce

2 pounds large shrimp, peeled and deveined
2 tablespoons low-sodium soy sauce
2 tablespoons fresh lemon or lime juice
1 tablespoon water
2 tablespoons brown sugar
1 teaspoon fresh grated ginger
1 clove garlic, crushed through a press
Peanut Sauce (recipe follows)
Hot cooked rice

Skewer the shrimp, putting about 4 or 5 on each skewer. Arrange in a shallow glass dish.

Combine soy sauce, lime or lemon juice, water, sugar, ginger and garlic. Pour over the shrimp and allow to marinate about 20 minutes or up to 2 hours.

Drain the shrimp and reserve the marinade.

Heat a grill to medium-low. Cook skewers for 5 to 6 minutes, basting occasionally with the Peanut Sauce. Do not overcook.

Serve hot with extra Peanut Sauce and white rice.

Makes 6 servings.

Peanut Sauce

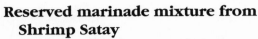

**Reserved marinade mixture from
  Shrimp Satay**
1 medium onion, diced (about 1 cup)
1 clove garlic, crushed through a press
1/4 teaspoon crushed hot red pepper
1/2 teaspoon curry powder
4 tablespoons coconut milk
6 tablespoons water
1/3 cup crunchy peanut butter

 Make the marinade and peanut sauce up to 1 week in advance and store in the refrigerator.

Pour the reserved marinade into a saucepan. Bring to a rolling boil and cook for 3 minutes. Stir in the chopped onion, garlic, red pepper, curry, coconut milk and water and simmer for 3 minutes longer.

Stir in the peanut butter. Cook, stirring frequently, over low heat until peanut butter is melted and sauce is thick and fragrant, about 3 to 5 minutes.

If mixture is too thick, add up to 3 more tablespoons of water.

Makes 2 cups or 8 servings.

Notes: Reheat the sauce in a microwave oven on medium (50 percent) power or on low heat on the stove. Sauce thickens as it cools; thin with additional water if necessary.

You can buy coconut milk in West Indian and Oriental markets. You can also make your own coconut milk by steeping the freshly grated meat of a whole coconut in boiling water. For every cup of coconut meat, use 2 cups of boiling water. Steep for 30 minutes, then squeeze out all the liquid and discard the coconut meat. The reserved liquid is the coconut milk.

Putting the cover on the barbecue grill allows the fish to absorb some of the smoky flavor. The sweetness in the barbecue sauce gives it balance.

Barbecued Salmon

2 pounds salmon fillets or steaks
2 tablespoons olive or canola oil
3 tablespoons ketchup
2 tablespoons molasses
1 tablespoon brown sugar
3 tablespoons lemon juice
3 tablespoons soy sauce
1 tablespoon prepared mustard
1 tablespoon red or white wine

 halibut, tuna, shark, swordfish

Heat a grill to medium-low. Brush the fillets or steaks with olive oil. Set aside.

In a small bowl, combine the ketchup, molasses, brown sugar, lemon juice, soy sauce, mustard and wine. Stir well. Place the salmon on the grill and baste lightly with the barbecue sauce. Cook with the grill covered for 4 to 5 minutes, basting occasionally.

If cooking skin-on fillets, cook on one side only for another 4 minutes. If cooking steaks, turn and cook covered on the other side for 4 minutes. Baste second side with barbecue sauce about every minute.

Makes 4 to 5 servings.

Notes: You may want to use a hinged grill basket to prevent the fish from sticking to the rack. This is a rich, sticky sauce.

This is a no-fail recipe — delicious every time. My husband is crazy about the taste of cooked pineapple.

Sweet-Tart Shrimp and Vegetable Kebabs

1 pound medium shrimp, shelled and deveined
1 (8-ounce) can pineapple chunks in natural juice
1 tablespoon reserved pineapple juice from can
2 tablespoons whole-grain mustard
2 tablespoons rice vinegar
1 tablespoon olive oil
2 tablespoons honey
1/4 teaspoon dried ginger
1 (8-ounce) can whole water chestnuts
1 red or green bell pepper, cut into wedges

cubed monkfish, cubed tuna or shark

In a medium-sized bowl, combine the mustard, rice vinegar, oil, honey, reserved pineapple juice and ginger. Stir well. Add the shrimp and toss to coat evenly. Refrigerate and allow the shrimp to marinate for up to 1 hour.

When ready to cook, thread the shrimp, pineapple chunks, water chestnuts and bell pepper on skewers. Brush vegetables lightly with remaining marinade.

Cook skewers on a medium-hot barbecue grill until shrimp are pink and vegetables are crisp-tender. Discard marinade.

Makes 6 servings.

Grilled Shark
with Spicy Orange Marmalade

1 1/4 pounds shark steaks, about 1-inch thick
1 cup orange juice
2 tablespoons lemon juice
2 cloves garlic, crushed through a press
1 small sweet onion, such as Florida, Vidalia or Walla Walla, diced (about 1/4 cup)
1/8 teaspoon crushed hot red pepper or a pinch of cayenne pepper
1/3 cup orange marmalade

 halibut, mahi mahi, mackerel with the skin on

Place the shark steaks in a shallow dish. Pour orange and lemon juice, garlic, onion and crushed pepper or cayenne over the steaks and refrigerate. Allow shark to marinate for 3 hours. (The fish can be marinated in the morning and cooked in the evening.)

When ready to cook, drain and reserve marinade. Cook fish on a barbecue grill over medium-high heat. Cook for 4 minutes on the first side; turn and cook for 3 minutes on the second side.

While shark is grilling, combine the marmalade with the reserved marinade in a small saucepan. Bring mixture to a boil, stirring occasionally. Cook for 3 to 4 minutes, until liquid is partially cooked away and mixture looks syrupy.

Serve a spoonful of the marmalade sauce over each shark steak and pass the rest separately.

Makes 5 servings.

Note: For a fresher flavor, mix a second batch of orange juice, lemon juice and garlic to boil with the marmalade for the sauce.

How to prepare fish

• Rinse fillets and steaks under cold, running water before cooking. Pat dry with paper towels and proceed with recipe.

• For safety, wash hands, cutting boards, knives and other utensils after cutting fish or shellfish.

• Don't mix raw fish or shellfish with lettuce, tomatoes or ingredients that will be eaten without cooking.

• Fish absorbs marinades much faster than beef or chicken. Delicate fish, such as perch or snapper, only need to marinate about 15 to 20 minutes. Firmer fish, such as mahi mahi, can marinate up to several hours. If necessary, you can place the fish in the marinade in the morning and cook it in the evening.

• Discard unused marinades. If you include it in a sauce for the fish, bring it to a boil and cook for at least 3 to 4 minutes before proceeding with the recipe.

• Some cookbooks call for soaking fish in milk before cooking. (They also call for soaking non-seafood items such as chicken and beef liver.) Soaking is supposed to sweeten the meat and remove strong flavors. It's an optional step.

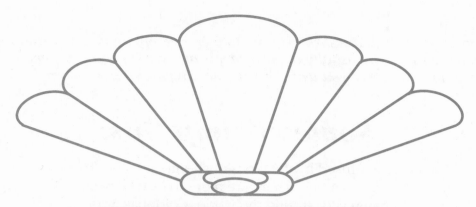

SHELLFISH

Popular shellfish are shrimp, crab, lobster, scallops, oysters, clams and mussels. They are usually in good supply at most seafood counters. If you don't see what you want, ask if you can place a special order.

Some shrimp tips:

• If you are confused by the types of shrimp at the seafood counter, you are not alone. There are more than 100 species of shrimp harvested commercially around the world. Color has nothing to do with taste, though most consumers gravitate toward pink shrimp. The shells and meat of all shrimp turn pink after cooking.

• Tiger shrimp: Farmed in large quantities in Thailand and Indonesia. They're usually a good buy. They are gray-green in color, with noticeable dark "tiger" stripes across the back.

• Northern white shrimp: Caught in large quantities in the Gulf of Mexico, especially off the coast of Louisiana. These shrimp are coral-colored with a thin, delicate shell and a black tail.

• Brown shrimp: Caught in large quantities in the Gulf of Mexico. These shrimp are coral colored with a fairly thick shell and a pink tail.

• Key West shrimp: Caught off the Keys, these shrimp are pale pink and have thin shells and pale tails.

• Pink Northern Shrimp: Caught in the waters of the Pacific Northwest and in the North Atlantic from Norway to Maine, the shells are pale pink and the meat appears mottled pink and white.

• White Shrimp and Whiteleg shrimp: Farmed in China and Ecuador, these shrimp have pale gray, thin shells and light pink or gray tails and legs.

• Prawns: Farm-raised freshwater shrimp. The term also refers to a small member of the lobster family. It's used fairly regularly on restaurant menus to describe large shrimp.

• Scampi: A term borrowed from an Italian word to describe small lobsters. On restaurant menus, scampi means shrimp that are cooked with garlic and butter or garlic and olive oil.

Buying shrimp:
• Frozen shrimp and frozen-and-thawed shrimp are often better quality than shrimp labeled as "fresh." Almost all shrimp are frozen before they reach the market.

• Ask to feel and smell a shrimp. It should be firm and not mushy. The shell should be intact and not torn or papery. It should have a faint salty smell.

• Avoid shrimp that have dark spots or loose shells.

• Shrimp are sold according to size. Size has nothing to do with how good the shrimp tastes, however larger shrimp cost more and entail less shelling.
Colossal or super-jumbo: 8 or less to a pound
Jumbo: 21 to 25 to a pound
Large: 36 to 40 to a pound
Medium: 61 to 70 to a pound
Small: 70 to 110 to a pound.

To shell shrimp:
• You can buy an inexpensive plastic shrimp peeler in many grocery stores or fish markets that pull off the shell and devein the shrimp in one step.
• To shell the shrimp by hand, hold the shrimp at the thick end and pull the swimmerets (the feathery legs on the underside) outward from the body.
• Scrape the shell off the back with your thumbnail and discard.
• For a showy presentation and appetizers, leave the tail flippers on the tail portion. For pasta, stir-fried dishes and baked entrees, remove the shells from the tail flippers.

To devein shrimp:
• It isn't necessary to remove the vein except in very large shrimp or for a showy presentation. The vein is the lower portion of the digestive tract, but it is tasteless and harmless.
• To remove the vein, use a small, stainless steel knife to cut a shallow incision down the entire length of the back. Use the tip of the knife to lift out the vein. Wipe the knife on a paper towel to get rid of the vein.
• To butterfly shrimp, cut a deep incision down the length of the body. Cut the shrimp almost but not quite in half. Lay cut-side up and fill the incision with a stuffing or sauce.

Rinsing and crisping shrimp:
• Soft shrimp can be made crisper by soaking in salted ice water for 10 to 15 minutes. Drain but don't rinse before cooking.
• Rinse shrimp in the shells before cooking. Drain thoroughly. Avoid rinsing shrimp after they have been shelled because they lose flavor and can absorb water.

Storing shrimp:
• Keep in the coldest part of the refrigerator for up to two days.
• Rinse in cold running water after second day.

Cooking shrimp:

• Shrimp are cooked as soon as they lose their translucence and turn pink. The meat curls like a half moon when cooked.
• If the meat curls all the way so the head portion touches the tail, the shrimp are overcooked.
• Do not overcook or the meat will be tough and tasteless.
• Follow cooking times and directions listed in individual recipes.

Other shellfish:

• Oysters, clams and mussels in the shell should be alive when you buy them. If the shells are slightly open, they should close when tapped. Discard those that don't close (after they're cooked, discard those that don't open.) Discard any that have broken shells.

Scallops:

• Most scallops are cleaned at sea. In the United States, only the pure, clean muscle meat is eaten. The color ranges from creamy white to pink.
• There are many species of scallop but they are classified in two broad groups — bay and sea.
• Bay scallops are tiny, about 1/2 inch in diameter. They average aboout 75 to 100 to a pound. The meat is very sweet and moist.
• Sea scallops are larger, about 1 to 1 1/2 inches in diameter. They average 25 to 30 to a pound. The meat is sweet but can become tough and rubbery if overcooked.
• Calico scallops are a tiny, exceptionally sweet variety, found in the Gulf of Mexico and off the east coast of Florida.
• The meat can be sauteed, grilled, poached, breaded and deep-fried or used in soups. Don't overcook.
• The bivalves have beautiful fan-shaped shells and are found in waters all over the world.

This is my favorite version of peel-and-eat shrimp for last-minute guests. Use at least one fresh herb to make this dish look pretty.

Herbed Steamed Shrimp

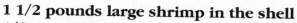

1 1/2 pounds large shrimp in the shell
1/2 cup water
1/4 cup white wine
4 whole peppercorns or 1/4 teaspoon pepper
1/4 teaspoon salt
3 tablespoons chopped fresh basil or 1/2 teaspoon dried
2 tablespoons chopped fresh thyme or 1/2 teaspoon dried
1 tablespoon chopped fresh dill or 1/4 teaspoon dried
Pinch of crushed red pepper

Combine the water, wine, peppercorns or pepper and herbs and red pepper in a shallow, 2-quart, microwave-safe dish. Cook on high (100 percent) power until the liquid is boiling. Stir and place shrimp in a single layer in dish. Cover with plastic wrap or wax paper. Cook on high (100 percent) power for 2 minutes. Stir to move shrimp from the outside of dish to the center. Cover and cook again on high (100 percent) power for 2 to 4 minutes, until shrimp are pink and curled.

(If some shrimp aren't fully cooked, remove them from the dish and cook them separately. That way all the shrimp won't be overcooked.)

Allow the shrimp to cool in the herb broth. Serve warm or chill until ready to serve.

Makes 4 to 8 servings.

Notes: Serve with Tarragon Cream Sauce, Curried Mayonnaise, Cocktail Sauce, Fresh Tartar Sauce or Make-Your-Own-Ranch Dressing. (See recipes in Extras chapter.)

Leeks are sweeter and milder than other kinds of onions. They're the perfect complement to the sea-sweet flavor of shrimp.

Leek and Shrimp Tart

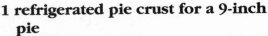

1 refrigerated pie crust for a 9-inch pie
1/2 pound shrimp, shelled and deveined
2 leeks (about 4 cups sliced)
2 tablespoons olive oil
1/2 teaspoon salt
1/4 teaspoon white pepper
1/4 teaspoon nutmeg
1/4 teaspoon sugar
2/3 cup half-and-half
2 eggs
1 cup shredded Jarlsberg or Swiss cheese

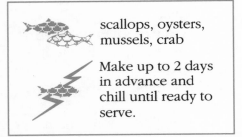

scallops, oysters, mussels, crab

Make up to 2 days in advance and chill until ready to serve.

Preheat oven to 350 F.

Press the pie crust into a 9-inch pie or quiche pan with a removable bottom.

Slice the leeks crosswise into 1/8-inch pieces, starting with the white part at the bottom. When you reach the green sections, remove the tough outer leaves and continue slicing tender, pale yellow portions. Watch for sand between the rings.

Heat the oil in a large, non-stick skillet. Over medium-low heat, fry the leeks for 8 to 10 minutes, stirring frequently until tender and transparent. Sprinkle evenly with salt, pepper, nutmeg and sugar and stir to blend well.

In a small bowl, whisk together the eggs and half-and-half. Spoon the leeks into the prepared pie crust. Arrange the shrimp on top and pour the egg mixture over all making sure it is evenly distributed among the leeks. Sprinkle evenly with the Jarlsberg or Swiss cheese. Bake for 30 to 35 minutes or until shrimp are pink and custard is firm. Serve warm or at room temperature.

Makes 6 servings or 12 appetizer portions.

This is colorful and flavorful enough to serve at a tropical dinner party. Get everything ready in advance because cooking only takes a minute.

Stir-Fried Shrimp with Mangoes

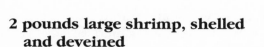

2 pounds large shrimp, shelled
  and deveined
2 tablespoons peanut or canola oil,
  divided
3/4 cup sliced green onions
4 ounces fresh mushrooms, sliced
1 large red bell pepper, cored,
  seeded and sliced thin
18 snow pea pods
1 large ripe mango, peeled and
  sliced or 10 prepared mango
  slices
1/4 cup cashew nuts
Hot cooked rice

Sauce:
1/2 teaspoon curry powder
1/8 teaspoon crushed red pepper
1 teaspoon grated fresh ginger
2 cloves garlic, crushed through a
  press
2 tablespoons frozen orange juice
  concentrate
2 tablespoons low-sodium soy
  sauce
2 tablespoons rice vinegar
1 cup clam juice or chicken broth
1 tablespoon cornstarch mixed to
  a paste with 1 tablespoon water

scallops, imitation
crab meat

Heat 1 tablespoon of the oil in a wok or large non-stick skillet. Briefly saute the shrimp until they are pink and curled. Remove from the pan and set aside. Don't overcook at this point because they will continue to cook later.

In a 2-cup measuring cup, mix the curry powder, crushed red pepper, ginger, garlic, orange juice, soy sauce, rice vinegar and chicken broth or clam juice. In a separate dish, combine the cornstarch and water.

Arrange all ingredients and vegetables near the stove.

Return the wok or skillet to the heat. When hot, add the remaining oil and add the green onions, mushrooms and red pepper and fry, stirring constantly for about 5 minutes. When the onions are soft, add the shrimp, snow peas and cashews to the wok or skillet. Cook about 2 minutes longer. Add the sauce ingredients and bring to a boil. Stir in the mango slices and the cornstarch paste. When the mixture comes to a boil, remove from heat immediately. Spoon over hot rice.

Makes 6 servings.

Cooking with Crab

There are hundreds of species of crabs. Most are interchangeable in cooking. The ones listed are some of the most common.

• Blue crab: One of the most common on the East Coast and found from Delaware to Florida. The meat is brown and white, and is mild and slightly sweet in flavor. Often available fresh or pasteurized.

• Snow crab and king crab: Found in cold Northern waters. The meat is white and very sweet. Often available frozen.

• Stone crab: Found in warm waters in the Gulf of Mexico and along the east coast of Florida and as far north as North Carolina. Usually, only the beautiful red and black-tipped claws are eaten. The season runs from October to May but frozen claws are available year-round.

• Dungeness crab: Found in the Pacific from Alaska to Mexico. It has succulent sweet meat and is available fresh or frozen.

• Soft-shell crab: Blue crabs that have molted their hard shells. They're in season from April to mid-September (with a peak in June and July). Frozen soft-shell crabs are available year-round.

Picked meat:

• Claw: Chunks of dark, flavorful meat. Usually the least expensive because of the color yet considered the most flavorful. The least likely to have bits of shell or cartilage. Use to make crab cakes.

• Lump or backfin: Large pieces of white meat from the body. Very sweet and usually expensive. Use to make salads and baked dishes.

• Special: Small pieces of white meat picked out from the body. Less expensive and the most likely to have bits of shell and cartilage. Use for stuffings.

• Pasteurized: Meat that has been treated with heat in the can at a high enough temperature to kill bacteria but not high enough to cook it. It can be stored in the refrigerator unopened for up to 6 months. Cook within 3 days of opening. Use in any recipe.

Frozen:

• Snow crab clusters and king crab legs are available frozen. Thaw in the refrigerator and steam over boiling water or bake until hot.

• Thaw frozen crab meat overnight in the refrigerator.

Louise Wainwright Simpson and her mother, Gerri, of Phoenix, Arizona, are two dear, lifelong friends. And they're both incredible cooks. Louise told me her mother found this recipe decades ago on the back of a potato chip bag. I reduced some of the calories from fat and made it in the microwave oven. It's still great.

Crab Chip Pie

Crust:
1 1/2 cups finely crushed potato chips (about 7 cups whole or 7 large handfuls)
1 green onion, chopped
1/3 cup melted butter or margarine
1 teaspoon paprika

Filling:
14 ounces frozen and thawed crab meat or pasteurized crab meat, flaked
3 tablespoons butter or margarine
1/2 cup diced green pepper (about 1/2 of a pepper)
1 small onion, finely diced (about 1/2 cup)
3 tablespoons flour
1/2 teaspoon salt
1/4 teaspoon white pepper
1/2 cup low-fat milk
1 (2-ounce) jar diced pimentos, drained
1 (4.25-ounce) can chopped ripe olives
1 tablespoon lemon juice
2 tablespoons chopped fresh parsley
1 cup light sour cream or imitation sour cream

Preheat oven to 375 F.

To make the potato chip crust, chop the green onion in the bowl of a food processor or blender. Add the potato chips and paprika and grind. While the machine is running, pour in the melted butter or margarine until the chips are pulverized. Reserve 1/3 cup of the mixture for later.

Press the mixture into six individual baking dishes. (Shell-shaped dishes give this a nice look.) Bake for 10 minutes, until brown around the edges. Cool. Reduce oven temperature to 350 F.

To make crab filling, melt the butter in a microwave-safe dish. Cook the onion and green pepper in the butter on high (100 percent) power for 1 to 2 minutes, or until the onion is soft. Stir in the flour, salt and pepper. Add the milk and cook on high (100 percent) power for 1 to 2 minutes until the mixture starts to boil and thicken. Stir and add the pimentos, olives, crab and parsley. Cook on high (100 percent) power for 1 to 2 minutes longer. Stir in sour cream and lemon juice and blend well.

Spoon the crab mixture into the prepared crusts. Sprinkle 1 tablespoon of reserved chip mixture over the filling. Bake for 20 minutes. (If using a single, large casserole dish, bake for 10 minutes longer.)

Makes 6 servings.

The crusts and filling can be prepared up to 1 day in advance and refrigerated separately. Assemble and bake the pies just before serving.

There are as many recipes for crab cakes as there are people in the Chesapeake Bay region. Norfolk-Style crab cakes have nothing added but butter and seasonings. Maryland-Style are less rich but more filling. Fry them in a cast-iron skillet but be careful because they're crumbly!

Maryland-Style Crab Cakes

1 pound pasteurized or frozen crab
  claw meat, thawed
1/4 cup half-and-half
3 tablespoons mayonnaise
1 egg, lightly beaten
1/4 teaspoon cayenne pepper
1 teaspoon dry mustard
1 tablespoon Worcestershire sauce
2 cups fresh, soft bread crumbs
2 green onions, finely chopped
6 tablespoons oil for frying

Make the crab cakes up to 8 hours in advance and layer them between sheets of wax paper. Refrigerate until ready to serve.

Pick through the crab meat to remove any bits of shell or cartilage. In a small container, mix together the half-and-half, mayonnaise, egg, cayenne pepper, mustard and Worcestershire. Combine the bread crumbs and green onions and stir in the egg mixture to make a sticky mixture. Shape into patties and separate them between sheets of wax paper.

Heat the oil in a skillet over medium-high heat. Fry without crowding the crab cakes for 7 minutes on the first side, flip gently with a slotted spatula and fry for 5 minutes on the second side. Keep warm until ready to serve.

Makes 8 crab cakes.

Notes: My friend and colleague, Linda Shrieves, whose father was born and raised on the Eastern Shore of Virginia, said purists fry the crab cakes in lard. They wouldn't dream of serving them with a sauce. However, these are terrific with Honey Mustard Sauce (recipe page 200)

There are many varieties of lobsters and none of them are inexpensive. Maine, or American lobster, is probably the costliest. For this excellent dish, the meat is pulled from the shell so you can save a little money by shopping for spiny or slipper lobsters.

Lobster Saute
with Sesame and Sugar Snap Peas

2 (5-ounce) lobster tails
1/4 pound sugar snap peas or snow
  peas
1 tablespoon peanut or canola oil
1 teaspoon minced fresh ginger
1 teaspoon Oriental sesame oil
2 tablespoons sesame seeds, toasted
1 tablespoon lemon juice

 scallops, monkfish, shrimp, shark nuggets.

Use kitchen scissors to cut the lobster tail in half down the belly. Pull out the meat. Discard the shells and cut the meat crosswise into 1/4-inch medallions.

Pull the stems off the sugar snap or snow peas and remove the strings, if any.

In a large, non-stick skillet, heat the peanut or canola oil over medium-high heat. Saute the ginger for 1 minute, until fragrant; add the lobster medallions. Saute for 2 minutes until the meat is white and opaque on one side. Add the snow peas and sesame seeds and stir to flip the medallions. Add the sesame oil and lemon juice. Stir and cook 2 minutes, allowing some of the liquid to evaporate as steam. Lobster is done when the meat is white and slightly curled. Don't overcook or it will be tough.

Makes 2 servings.

Notes: Sugar snap peas, also called sugar peas, are a cross between snow peas and English peas. The plump bright-green pods are completely edible. You can substitute snow peas.

To toast sesame seeds, bake in an ungreased pan in a 325 F oven for 4 to 5 minutes, checking frequently to prevent burning. Or toast them in an ungreased skillet over medium-low heat for 4 to 5 minutes, stirring frequently.

This is excellent served over fresh spinach as a warm lobster salad.

Zellwood, a small town northeast of Orlando, holds an annual Sweet Corn Festival at the end of May and calls itself the sweet corn capital of the world. Indeed, the yellow and white corn from Zellwood seems sweeter and crisper than any other kind.

Zellwood Corn and Gulf Shrimp Custard

3 ears white or yellow sweet corn or 1 (10-ounce) box frozen corn kernels, thawed
1/2 pound medium shrimp, shelled
1 tablespoon butter
2 green onions, chopped
1 clove garlic, crushed through a press
1/2 teaspoon salt
1/4 teaspoon pepper
Pinch crushed red pepper
1 tablespoon chopped fresh parsley
1/2 teaspoon rubbed sage
3 eggs
1/2 cup half-and-half

scallops, rock shrimp, clams

Use frozen shelled and deveined cooked shrimp in this recipe. They are available in the frozen foods section of most grocery stores. Thaw and drain before using.

Remove the kernels from the corn using a small, sharp knife. Hold the ear upright with one end in a deep bowl. Run the sharp edge of the blade away from you down the ear of corn. Turn the knife over and use the dull side of the blade to scrape out all the milky juices and pulp.

Use 1 tablespoon of the butter to grease a 1-quart baking dish. Set aside. Preheat oven to 350 F.

In a food processor or blender, combine the corn, green onions, garlic, salt, pepper, parsley and sage. Process once briefly to mix. Add the shrimp and eggs and process long enough to chop the shrimp but not puree them. Add the half-and-half. Blend long enough to mix the ingredients, but not puree them. Pour into the prepared baking dish and bake for 30 minutes, or until the custard is set. Remove from oven and allow to stand about 10 minutes before serving.

Makes 4 servings.

Notes: To prepare this in a microwave-oven proceed with recipe but pour into a microwave-safe dish. Cover with wax paper and cook on medium (50 percent) power for 12 minutes, giving dish a one-quarter turn every 4 minutes. Center will appear moist and loose but will set upon standing. If center is still liquid at the end of the cooking time, cook on medium (50 percent) power for up to 4 minutes longer. Allow to stand 5 minutes before serving.

If possible, use roasted red peppers in this recipe. The smoky flavor is the perfect complement to the sweet crab meat. Serve as an appetizer or round out the meal with salad and a vegetable.

Crab Cups

12 ounces pasteurized crab meat

2 tablespoons olive oil, divided

3 green onions, diced (about 1 cup)

1 (4-ounce) jar diced pimentos or 1 red pepper, roasted, peeled and diced

1 cup soft bread crumbs, loosely packed

1/2 teaspoon oregano or thyme leaves

1/2 teaspoon salt

1/4 teaspoon white pepper

1/4 teaspoon sugar

1 cup whipping cream

4 tablespoons dry sherry

 imitation crab, shrimp, lobster, scallops

Preheat oven to 350 F.

Brush four ramekins or custard cups with 1 teaspoon of the olive oil. Place remaining oil in a non-stick skillet over medium heat. Fry green onions until soft, about 3 minutes. Add crab, pimento, bread crumbs, oregano, salt, white pepper and sugar. Stir well to combine. Pour cream and sherry over mixture and stir to moisten well. Bring to a boil and cook 1 to 2 minutes until bread is soft.

Transfer crab to prepared cups. Bake for 20 minutes, or until brown on top.

Makes 4 servings.

Notes: These can be made in advance and frozen for up to one month before baking. Bake from the frozen state and add 15 to 20 minutes to the cooking time. This also can be made in a 1-quart souffle dish.

True paella is the glory of Spanish cooking but it takes hours to chop the vegetables and brown the meats. This version uses packaged, Spanish-style yellow rice and shrimp. The shellfish steam on top of the rice as it cooks. Serve it with a light red wine and tossed salad.

15-Minute Paella

1 (8-ounce) package Spanish yellow rice mix, such as Vigo
1/2 pound shrimp, shelled
1 (4-ounce) jar diced pimentos
1 cup frozen green peas
2 tablespoons dry sherry
1/4 teaspoon salt

Start the rice according to package directions. Boil rice for 5 minutes, then reduce heat to a simmer. Spread the shrimp and pimentos in an even layer on top of the rice. Cover and cook for 10 minutes longer.

When the water has almost been absorbed, turn off the heat. Sprinkle the frozen peas on top. Cover and allow to stand for 5 minutes. Sprinkle with sherry and salt. Stir.

Serve hot.

Makes 4 servings.

Cholesterol in shellfish:

• The cholesterol content of shellfish has been revised downward drastically because of errors in the way cholesterol content was measured. Former measuring methods included all types of sterols, of which cholesterol is only one. Newer research has shown that eating shellfish is no more likely to raise blood cholesterol levels than eating lean meat or skinless poultry.

• Shellfish is low in saturated fat. Saturated fat is more closely linked to a rise in blood cholesterol levels than dietary cholesterol is.

• *Cholesterol in a 4-ounce serving of shellfish:*

	Cholesterol (mg)	Calories from fat	total calories
Clams	39	10	85
Crab (Alaskan king)	48	6	96
Crab (Dungeness)	67	10	98
Crawfish	159	11	102
Lobster (Northern)	109	9	103
Lobster (spiny)	80	16	128
Mussels (blue)	32	23	98
Oysters (Eastern)	63	26	79
Scallops	38	8	101
Shrimp	174	17	121
Squid	266	15	105

Source: United States Department of Agriculture

Shrimp, Artichokes and Sun-Dried Tomatoes on Seasoned Rice

1 (10-ounce) package broccoli and herb flavored rice pilaf mix
24 medium shrimp, shelled and deveined
1 clove garlic, crushed through a press
2 teaspoons olive oil
1/3 cup chopped sun-dried tomatoes, packed in oil or dehydrated
1/2 teaspoon dried basil
2 tablespoons white wine or liquid from soaking the sun-dried tomatoes
1 (10-ounce) box frozen artichokes, thawed

Cook the rice pilaf 20 minutes according to package directions.

If using dehydrated sun-dried tomatoes, soak in hot water for 10 minutes until soft. Drain and chop into pieces. Sun-dried tomatoes packed in oil don't need to be soaked.

While the rice is cooking, place the oil and garlic in a microwave-safe baking dish. Cook on high (100 percent) power for 1 minute. Stir in the shrimp, tomatoes, basil and wine. Coat the shrimp evenly with the herbs and oil. Cook on high (100 percent) power for 2 minutes. Push all the shrimp to the center of the dish. Spread the artichokes around the outside of the dish. Cook on high (100 percent) power for 5 minutes longer, stirring every 2 minutes, until shrimp are pink and curled. Allow to stand at room temperature for 2 minutes.

Spoon the shrimp mixture over the hot, seasoned rice.

Makes 4 servings.

Notes: Other varieties of rice also taste great in this dish. Even plain white rice tastes good with this topping!

I first tasted a version of these crunchy shrimp at the snazzy Peabody Orlando hotel, where they were served as appetizers for banquets.

Coconut Shrimp

24 jumbo shrimp
1/4 cup flour
1/2 teaspoon salt
1/2 teaspoon sugar
2 eggs
2 tablespoons milk
2 dashes liquid hot sauce
2 cups shredded coconut
2/3 cup peanut oil

Shell the shrimp but leave the tails attached if possible. Butterfly down the back and remove the vein, if any.

In a bowl, beat together the eggs, milk and hot sauce. Combine the flour, salt and sugar on a separate plate. Put the coconut in a bowl.

Hold each shrimp by the tail, dip in the flour and shake off any excess. Dip in the egg mixture, then roll in coconut to coat thickly. Make sure the coconut adheres to the shrimp. Place on waxed paper and refrigerate until ready to cook.

Heat the oil in a large skillet over medium-high heat. Fry the shrimp without crowding on one side until golden. Turn with tongs or a slotted spoon and fry on second side.

Place on several thicknesses of paper towels and keep warm in a 200-degree oven until all are done. Serve plain or with Pepper Jelly Sauce (recipe page 8) or Cocktail Sauce (recipe page 196).

Makes 24 appetizer servings.

Notes: The swiftest (and neatest) way to dip and coat the shrimp is to use two hands. Use your left hand to dip the shrimp in the flour and egg mixtures and your right hand to dip the shrimp in the coconut.

These can be dipped in advance and frozen for up to one month before cooking. Cook frozen but make sure the oil stays hot. If the oil gets too cool, the shrimp will be greasy.

Danish Blue cheese, also called Danablu, is milder than French Roquefort and more complex than American blue cheeses. Most grocery stores carry it. The flavor accents the shellfish but doesn't overpower it.

Baked Ramekins of Seafood with Danish Blue Cheese

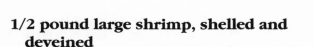

1/2 pound large shrimp, shelled and deveined
1/2 pound sea or bay scallops
2 tablespoons unsalted butter
2 tablespoons flour
1/2 teaspoon salt
1/4 teaspoon white pepper
1/8 teaspoon nutmeg
1/2 cup milk
1/2 cup whipping cream
1/4 cup white wine or dry sherry
2 to 3 ounces Danish blue or other blue cheese
1 egg yolk
1 cup loosely packed fresh bread crumbs

 all shrimp, all scallops, shucked oysters, cubed fish

Preheat the oven to 375 F.

In a large saucepan, melt the butter and stir in the flour, salt, pepper and nutmeg. Cook for 1 minute, until flour mixture is bubbling. Gradually stir in milk and cream. Stir until mixture comes to a boil and thickens. Stir in wine or sherry and cheese. Cook, stirring gently, for 2 minutes or until cheese is melted. Add the shellfish and cook 1 minute longer. Remove from heat.

In a separate bowl, whisk the egg yolk. Pour a small amount of the hot sauce into the egg yolk to warm it, then pour the yolk back into the sauce. (Warming the yolk with the sauce helps keep the egg from scrambling when it hits the hot sauce.)

Divide the sauce and shellfish mixture between 4 ramekins or au gratin dishes. Sprinkle with crumbs. Bake for 15 to 20 minutes, until sauce is bubbling.

Makes 4 servings.

Broiled Scallops with Gruyere

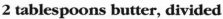

2 tablespoons butter, divided
1 tablespoon olive oil
1 small yellow onion, minced (about 1/4 cup)
2 cloves garlic, crushed through a press
1 pound sea or bay scallops
1/4 cup white wine
1 cup fresh soft bread crumbs, loosely packed
1/2 cup shredded Gruyere cheese, loosely packed
2 tablespoons fresh parsley, chopped, or 1/2 teaspoon dried

 oysters, shrimp, squid, mussels, medallions of lobster

Preheat oven broiler.

Arrange 4 large scallop shells or small au gratin dishes on a baking sheet. Set aside.

In a large, non-stick skillet, melt 1 tablespoon of the butter and olive oil together. When the butter foams, add the yellow onion and saute 2 minutes until soft. Add the garlic and scallops and stir to blend ingredients. Saute over medium-high heat for 2 to 3 minutes, until the scallops begin to look opaque.

Add the white wine and bring mixture to a simmer. Cook for 3 minutes longer. Spoon scallop mixture and cooking juices into shells or au gratin dishes.

In a separate bowl, mix together the bread crumbs, Gruyere cheese and parsley. Melt remaining 1 tablespoon of butter. Pour over crumb mixture and toss well. Spoon crumbs over and around scallops, so the bread absorbs the cooking juices.

(Recipe can be prepared ahead at this point and refrigerated several hours or until ready to serve.)

Broil about 4 inches from the heat element, about 4 minutes, or until the crumbs are golden and the cheese has melted.

Makes 4 servings.

Whether these Mexican-style cheese crisps are folded and eaten like a soft taco or carved with a knife and fork, they have a wonderful, earthy flavor.

Oyster and Black Bean Quesadillas

24 shucked oysters
1 tablespoon canola oil
6 corn tortillas
1/2 cup diced tomato (about 1/2
    medium tomato)
1/2 cup finely chopped fresh cilantro
2 green onions, diced
4 ounces Monterey Jack cheese, grated
    (about 1 1/2 cups)
4 ounces sharp Cheddar cheese,
    grated (about 1 1/2 cups)
1 (14-ounce) can black beans, rinsed
    and drained
Salsa
Sour cream

 scallops, shrimp or smoked oysters. Don't precook smoked oysters.

Place the oil in a non-stick skillet and saute the oysters over medium-low heat. Cook for 2 to 3 minutes only. Remove from pan and set aside. (Oysters will cook more under the broiler, so don't overcook them at this stage.)

Arrange the corn tortillas on a baking sheet. Sprinkle each tortilla evenly with the Monterey Jack cheese, tomatoes, cilantro, green onions and beans. Arrange oysters on top. Sprinkle the Cheddar cheese over the oysters.

Preheat the oven broiler and cook the quesadillas until the cheese is melted and the tortillas are brown around the edge. The quesadillas can be kept warm in a 200 F oven for 10 minutes before serving.

Top with salsa and serve with a dollop of sour cream, if desired.

Makes 6 servings.

Smooth and sinfully delicious.

Scallops Mistral

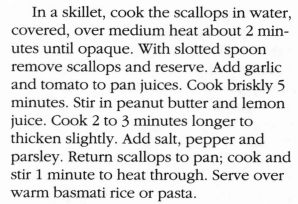

1 pound sea scallops, sliced in half widthwise if large
1/2 cup water
1 large clove garlic, crushed through a press
1 large tomato, seeded and chopped
1 tablespoon creamy peanut butter
1 tablespoon lemon juice
1/4 teaspoon salt
Dash white pepper
1 tablespoon parsley, chopped
Cooked Basmati rice or pasta

In a skillet, cook the scallops in water, covered, over medium heat about 2 minutes until opaque. With slotted spoon remove scallops and reserve. Add garlic and tomato to pan juices. Cook briskly 5 minutes. Stir in peanut butter and lemon juice. Cook 2 to 3 minutes longer to thicken slightly. Add salt, pepper and parsley. Return scallops to pan; cook and stir 1 minute to heat through. Serve over warm basmati rice or pasta.

Makes 4 servings.

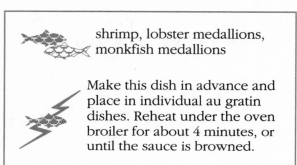

shrimp, lobster medallions, monkfish medallions

Make this dish in advance and place in individual au gratin dishes. Reheat under the oven broiler for about 4 minutes, or until the sauce is browned.

Garlic is the secret to this outstanding dish.

Scampi

24 jumbo shrimp, shelled
Juice of 1 lemon, about 3 tablespoons
6 tablespoons unsalted butter
2 tablespoons olive oil
4 cloves garlic, crushed through a press
2 tablespoons finely chopped fresh parsley
1/4 cup dry white wine or vermouth
1/8 teaspoon white pepper
3 cups hot cooked rice, pasta or noodles

Butterfly the shrimp by slicing through the backs from tip to tail. Remove the dark vein, if any. In a large skillet, melt the butter and olive oil together. When the mixture starts to foam, add the shrimp and garlic. Cook, stirring frequently for 2 to 3 minutes. Add the parsley, pepper and wine. Bring mixture to a boil, stirring constantly for 3 minutes. Serve immediately over hot rice, pasta or noodles.

Makes 4 servings.

A great blend of flavors and textures. Double the sauce mixture if you want it to soak into the rice.

Stir-Fried Lemon Shrimp

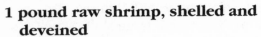

1 pound raw shrimp, shelled and deveined
1 lemon
3 tablespoons soy sauce
3 tablespoons brown sugar
1 tablespoon cornstarch
1 tablespoon water
1 clove garlic, crushed through a press
2 tablespoons canola oil
3 green onions, sliced on the diagonal into 1/2-inch pieces
1 medium red bell pepper, cut into strips (about 1 cup)
8 ounces fresh mushrooms, sliced (about 3 cups)
1 (5-ounce) can water chestnuts, sliced
4 ounces snow peas, stems removed
Cooked rice

 scallops, squid rings, chunks of tuna or swordfish

Use a vegetable peeler to remove the colored yellow part of the lemon rind. Try not to get too much of the white pith underneath. Slice the rind into matchstick pieces. Soak in a small dish of ice water.

Squeeze the lemon until you get 4 tablespoons of juice. (You can add bottled lemon juice to make the total amount if necessary.)

In a small dish, combine the lemon juice, soy sauce, brown sugar, cornstarch, water and garlic. Stir until the sugar has dissolved and no lumps of cornstarch remain. Set aside.

Heat the oil in a wok or non-stick skillet. Oil should be very hot before adding shrimp. Cook the shrimp, stirring constantly until they begin to curl. Remove from the wok, leaving as much oil as possible in the pan. (The shrimp will continue to cook, so don't leave them in the pan too long.)

Drain the lemon peel. Add it, the green onions and red pepper to the wok or skillet. Cook, stirring constantly for 3 to 4 minutes. Add the mushrooms, water chestnuts, snow peas and shrimp to the pan. Cook for 3 minutes longer, until the mushrooms are dark and the snow peas are bright green.

Stir the lemon and cornstarch mixture and pour it into the hot wok. Stir to coat all the vegetables. Allow the sauce to thicken, then remove immediately from heat.

Serve over hot, freshly cooked rice.
Makes 6 servings.

Tarpon Springs is a charming little community on the Gulf Coast of Florida that was founded in the early 1900s by Greek sponge fishermen. The town, which inspired this dish, is still famous for great Greek seafood.

Tarpon-Springs Style Greek Shrimp with Rice

20 extra-large shrimp
4 medium plum or roma tomatoes
3 large cloves garlic, crushed through a press
1 tablespoon olive oil
1 teaspoon dried oregano
1/8 teaspoon crushed red pepper
2 tablespoons fresh parsley, minced or 1 teaspoon dried parsley
1 cup long-grain rice
1/2 cup dry white wine
1/4 teaspoon salt
1 cup hot water
2 ounces feta cheese, crumbled
Fresh lemon wedges for garnish

 squid rings, scallops, clams, oysters

Preheat oven to 325 F. Spray 4 individual casserole dishes with non-stick cooking spray or coat lightly with olive oil. You can substitute a 1-quart casserole dish.

Assemble all the ingredients near the stove.

Shell the shrimp and remove the dark vein, if any. Set aside. Core the tomatoes and slice lengthwise. Squeeze out the seeds. Dice.

Heat the olive oil in a large skillet and stir in the crushed garlic and the shrimp. Cook for 1 to 2 minutes, stirring occasionally, until the shrimp begin to curl and look pink. Don't overcook them at this stage because they continue to cook.

Stir in the tomatoes, oregano, red pepper, parsley, salt and rice. Make sure the rice gets well-coated. Stir in the wine and cook until it comes to a boil. Remove from heat and divide the mixture between the prepared casserole dishes or place all in the 1-quart dish. Divide the water between the dishes and stir well. Sprinkle with feta cheese.

Bake for 15 to 20 minutes or until liquid has been absorbed. Serve with garnish of lemon wedges.

Makes 4 servings.

This vibrant Thai salad can be prepared in advance and dressed with it's chili-spiked dressing right before serving. In the summer use fresh apricots, but canned apricots in light syrup work also.

Fresh Apricot Thai Salad

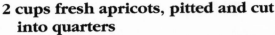

2 cups fresh apricots, pitted and cut into quarters
3/4 pound cooked, shelled shrimp
1 medium cucumber, peeled
1 cup bean sprouts, rinsed and patted dry
Bibb lettuce for lining plates
1/4 cup rice vinegar
2 teaspoons sugar
1/4 cup canola oil
1/2 teaspoon chili oil (available at Oriental markets and many grocery stores)
2 tablespoons coarsely chopped peanuts
3 tablespoons fresh cilantro, finely chopped
1 lime, cut into wedges

 scallops, imitation crab

Slice the cucumber in half lengthwise and use a spoon to scrape out the seeds. Slice lengthwise into thin matchsticks. Arrange the lettuce in the bottom of a serving bowl or shallow platter. Top with the apricots, cucumber, shrimp and bean sprouts. Cover and refrigerate until ready to serve. In a jar with a tight-fitting lid, combine vinegar, sugar, and the canola and chili oils. Shake vigorously to blend. Just before serving, sprinkle salad with peanuts and cilantro. Dress and serve with lime wedges.

Makes 4 servings.

Notes: If you can't find fresh apricots, use a 6-ounce package dried apricots. Soak the fruit in water until plump, then pat dry and slice into halves or quarters.

Risotto is a specialty of Venice, where the dish is prepared with a variety of foods, including seafood, mushrooms, sausage, ham and vegetables. This version makes a great main course with a salad and a glass of Italian white wine.

Garlic and Lemon Risotto with Shrimp

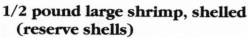

1/2 pound large shrimp, shelled (reserve shells)
5 cups water
1 (8-ounce) bottle clam juice
1/4 teaspoon salt
1 head garlic, unpeeled and coarsely chopped
2 tablespoons olive oil
1 small onion or 2 shallots, chopped
2 cloves garlic, peeled and crushed through a press
1 cup Arborio rice
1/4 cup dry white wine
1/4 teaspoon white pepper
Juice of 1/2 lemon (2 to 3 tablespoons)
1 teaspoon lemon zest, freshly grated
1/4 cup Parmesan cheese, freshly grated
1/2 cup black or green olives, preferably Italian, French or Greek, pitted

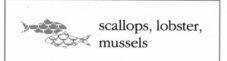
scallops, lobster, mussels

Notes: Arborio is a short-grained Italian rice that can absorb a great deal of liquid without falling apart or getting mushy. It is available at Italian markets, specialty food stores and through mail-order catalogs, such as Williams-Sonoma.

In a large, heavy saucepan, bring water, clam juice, salt, shrimp shells, and coarsely chopped head of garlic to a boil. Reduce heat, cover and simmer for 20 minutes. Pour the liquid through a colander and strain out the shells and garlic. Discard. (The broth can be prepared several days in advance and refrigerated until ready to cook.)

Pour the broth into a measuring cup to equal 4 cups. Set it aside.

Heat the oil in a large saucepan. Add the onion or shallots. Cook, stirring frequently, until vegetables are transparent, about 3 minutes. Add the remaining 2 cloves of garlic and the rice to the saucepan, stirring to coat every grain with oil and onion flavor. Stir in the white wine and adjust heat so it bubbles but does not evaporate too quickly.

Add 1 cup of the broth to the rice. Stir frequently to keep rice from sticking and to keep liquid distributed. Continue stirring and adding the garlic water by cupfuls until there is only 1/2 cup left. This will take about 20 to 25 minutes. Rice should be creamy-looking but tender. Pit the olives if necessary and cut into halves. Stir the white pepper, lemon juice and lemon zest into the remaining 1/2 cup of broth. Stir mixture into the rice and cook for 1 to 2 more minutes.

Add half of the Parmesan cheese and the olives and stir again.

Remove from heat and serve immediately. Sprinkle with remaining cheese.

Makes 4 servings.

Crunchy fennel and licorice liqueur give this shrimp dish a distinctive flavor. Fennel is usually available in markets from fall through spring.

Shrimp with Fennel

2 pounds shrimp, shelled
1 cup snow peas
4 tablespoons olive oil
3 onions, chopped
2 cloves garlic
**1 bulb fennel, trimmed, quartered and
    sliced**
1 red bell pepper, sliced
1/2 cup chicken broth
**1/4 cup licorice liqueur, such as
    anisette or Pernod**
1/2 teaspoon ground cardamom
1 lime, juiced
Cooked orzo or rice

scallops, lobster

Wash and snap stems off snow peas. Cook in the microwave oven on high (100 percent) power for 1 minute. Rinse under cold water. Drain.

In a large skillet or in a microwave-safe dish, heat the olive oil. Cook the onions and garlic until they are soft but not brown. Add the fennel and red pepper and cook for 3 to 4 minutes longer. Add the chicken broth, licorice liqueur, cardamom and lime juice. Reduce heat, cover and cook for 10 minutes. Stir in the shrimp and cook for 5 minutes longer, until the shrimp are pink and curled.

Stir in the snow peas. Serve over orzo or rice.

Makes 8 servings.

Make this quasi-Oriental dish with either fresh or frozen vegetables; frozen vegetables don't need to be blanched or defrosted before cooking. Have the sauce and ingredients at hand before turning on the stove because cooking only takes minutes.

Eight-Ingredient Fried Rice

Sauce:

3 tablespoons low-sodium soy sauce

2 tablespoons water

2 tablespoons rice vinegar

1 tablespoon oyster or hoisin sauce

1 tablespoon ketchup

1 teaspoon sugar

1 clove garlic, crushed through a
   press

Rice:

2 tablespoons oil

1 small yellow onion, sliced into
   strips

1 1/2 cups celery, cut on the diagonal

1 cup carrots, cut on the diagonal

1 cup shrimp, shelled

1 cup sea scallops, sliced in half
   widthwise, or whole bay scallops

1/2 cup red or green bell pepper,
   diced

3 cups cooked, cooled rice (preferably
   day old)

1 cup sugar snap peas or snow peas,
   stems removed

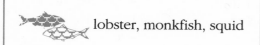 lobster, monkfish, squid

Combine all the ingredients for the sauce in a 2-cup mixing bowl. Stir vigorously with a fork until the sugar has dissolved. Place near the stove where it will be handy.

Assemble the remaining ingredients near the stove in individual piles or dishes. Precook the carrots for 1 minute in a microwave oven on high (100 percent) power. The carrots may also be blanched in boiling water for 2 minutes to tenderize them.

Place the oil in a wok or a large skillet. Set over high heat and allow oil to become quite hot. Add the onions first, stirring occasionally until they begin to caramelize and turn brown around the edges. Add the celery and stir for 2 minutes longer. Add the carrots, shrimp and scallops, and bell pepper and cook for 2 minutes longer, stirring constantly.

Add the rice all at once, stirring quickly to mix all ingredients together. (Some rice may begin to stick to the sides of the wok or skillet, but continue stirring.) Add the sugar snap peas and pour in sauce mixture. Stir until mixture is evenly colored brown with the sauce. Remove from heat and serve immediately.

Makes 4 servings.

One banana adds a touch of tropical sweetness to this low-fat, low-calorie entree. Onions, garlic, thyme and roasted peanuts add a savory balance to this Caribbean-inspired blend.

Sunshine Stuffed Peppers
with Shrimp and Banana

4 red, yellow or green peppers
2 teaspoons olive oil
1 medium onion, peeled and chopped
1 to 2 cloves garlic, chopped
2 medium, ripe tomatoes, seeded and
    chopped
1/2 cup rice, uncooked
1 (8-ounce) bottle of clam juice or fish
    stock
1/4 cup water
Salt to taste
3/4 pound shrimp, shelled and
    deveined
2 tablespoons parsley, chopped
1 tablespoon fresh thyme, chopped or
    1/4 teaspoon dried thyme
1 ripe banana, peeled and chopped
2 teaspoons fresh lime juice
3 tablespoons roasted peanuts,
    coarsely chopped
1/2 cup water

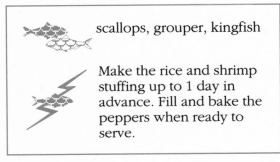

scallops, grouper, kingfish

Make the rice and shrimp stuffing up to 1 day in advance. Fill and bake the peppers when ready to serve.

Preheat oven to 350 F.

In a large skillet, heat olive oil over medium-high heat. Add onions and cook, stirring occasionally for 4 to 5 minutes. Add garlic and tomatoes, stirring well. Cook until tomatoes begin to exude liquid. Add rice, clam juice, water and salt and stir well. Bring to a boil, reduce heat to a simmer; cover. Cook until rice has absorbed most of the liquid, about 12 minutes. Add shrimp and cook until they begin to curl and look opaque, about 3 minutes longer. Shrimp will continue to cook in the oven. Remove from heat and set aside.

Wash peppers and slice off the stem end. Remove the stems and finely chop the surrounding pepper flesh. Add to the rice mixture. If necessary, cut the bottom of the peppers so they stand upright. Stir in the parsley, thyme, chopped banana, lime juice and roasted peanuts to the rice mixture.

Stuff the peppers. Place in a baking dish. Pour the remaining 1/2 cup water around the peppers and bake for 30 to 35 minutes.

Makes 4 servings.

Notes: When shopping for peppers look for those that have a uniform shape and flat bottoms so they will stand upright and look attractive on the plate. The stuffing also can be baked separately and served in a casserole with a lattice of peppers criss-crossed over the top. For a spicier blend, add a little minced jalapeno or serrano chili.

These New Orleans-style flavors will put music in your soul.

Bourbon Street Shrimp

4 tablespoons butter
2 tablespoons olive oil
2 medium potatoes, peeled and finely
　　diced
1/2 cup whole button mushrooms,
　　wiped clean and stems removed
1/3 cup white wine
2 cloves garlic, finely chopped or
　　crushed through a press
2 pounds shrimp, shelled and
　　deveined
1/4 teaspoon salt
1/8 teaspoon nutmeg
1/8 teaspoon white pepper
Pinch chopped fresh parsley
1 cup green peas
Cooked rice or noodles

In a non-stick skillet, melt butter and olive oil. When the butter is hot, add the potatoes. Reduce heat to low. Cook the potatoes until they begin to turn golden, stirring frequently. Place the mushrooms in the pan stem-side up and cook for 5 minutes. Stir. Pour in the wine and garlic. Increase heat until the wine mixture begins to simmer. Add the shrimp, salt, nutmeg and white pepper. Cover and allow mixture to simmer gently for 5 minutes. Add the peas and parsley and heat through.

Serve with rice or noodles.

Makes 4 servings.

Round out this elegant and easy dish with a big salad loaded with veggies and a bottle of good white wine. This is a winner.

Stuffed Lobster with Crab

2 (7-to 12-ounce) lobster tails
1/2 pound pasteurized crab meat, picked through to remove shell and cartilage
1/2 cup dry unseasoned bread crumbs
4 tablespoons unsalted butter, melted
3 tablespoons finely chopped fresh parsley
4 tablespoons finely chopped fresh basil or 1/2 teaspoon dried basil
3 green onions, finely chopped
2 tablespoons lemon juice
3 dashes of hot sauce or 1/4 teaspoon cayenne pepper
1 egg lightly beaten

Preheat oven to 400 F.

Using a large sharp or serrated knife, slice lobster tails in half lengthwise. Reserve any juice. Use a sharp paring knife to cut away the membranes holding the meat in the shell. Remove the meat and reserve the shells.

Chop the lobster into bite-sized pieces. Combine the meat in a bowl. Add the crab, bread crumbs, butter, herbs, onions, lemon juice, hot sauce and egg. Stir to make a slightly moist stuffing. Add any reserved juice from the lobster. Lightly fill each halved lobster shell with stuffing. Refrigerate.

Pour about 1/2 cup of water in the bottom of an oven-proof baking dish. Arrange the lobsters in the pan so they don't tip but aren't submerged. Bake for 12 to 15 minutes until the shells are bright red and the surface is golden brown.

Makes 4 servings.

Tastes like New England clam chowder without the soup.

Easy Clam Pie

3 slices bacon, chopped
1 slice lean ham, diced
1 large onion, chopped
1 large baking potato, diced
1 teaspoon thyme leaves
Freshly ground black pepper to taste
1 pint chopped clams with liquor
1 cup clam juice (or reserved clam liquor with water added)
2 tablespoons quick cooking tapioca
2 refrigerated 9-inch pie crusts

 canned clams

Preheat oven to 400 F.

Fry the bacon until crisp. Drain off all but 2 tablespoons of bacon fat and add the ham, onion and potatoes. Fry until onion is soft, about 6 minutes. Add the thyme and pepper. Set aside.

Drain the clams and reserve the liquid. Stir the clams, clam liquor and water or clam juice and tapioca into a saucepan. Bring to a simmer and cook for 5 minutes until mixture thickens. Stir in the potatoes, ham and bacon. Set aside.

Place the crust in a 9-inch pie pan. Pour tapioca-clam mixture into crust. Lay the second crust over the clam mixture. Pinch edges together to seal and crimp to form a decorative border. Cut a vent for steam in the center.

Bake in center of the oven for 20 minutes. Reduce heat to 350 F and bake 20 minutes longer until pastry is brown and crisp. Serve warm.

Makes 14 appetizer servings or 6 main course servings.

Note: This recipe freezes like a champ.

Anybody who likes fajitas will love these. In Mexico, the word fajita means "little ribbon or sash" because the meat is cut in narrow strips.

Seafarer's Fajitas

Pico de Gallo (recipe follows) or
  commercial salsa
Grated Cheddar or Monterey Jack
  cheese
Chopped tomatoes
Sour cream or sour half-and-half
Flour tortillas
1 pound bay scallops
1 pound medium shrimp, shelled and
  deveined
2 tablespoons olive oil
1 sweet onion, such as Vidalia, sliced
  into strips
1 red or green bell pepper, sliced into
  strips
1/4 cup lime juice
2 tablespoons apple-cider vinegar
3 tablespoons brown sugar
2 cloves garlic, crushed through a
  press
1 tablespoon Worcestershire sauce

Combine the lime juice, vinegar, brown sugar, garlic and Worcestershire and pour over the bay scallops and shrimp. Allow to marinate for 10 to 15 minutes.

Arrange the salsa or Pico de Gallo, cheese, tomatoes, sour cream and flour tortillas on the table or where you plan to serve. Once you start cooking, the recipe is done quickly.

In a large, non-stick skillet, heat the olive oil. Add the onion and saute over medium-high heat. Cook for 2 to 3 minutes then add the red bell pepper. Cook, stirring occasionally for 2 to 3 minutes longer. Onion should just begin to turn golden along the edges.

Drain the lime marinade off the seafood and pour half into the skillet with the onion and pepper. Discard remaining marinade.

Bring the mixture to a boil and cook until the liquid is reduced to 2 tablespoons.

Add the seafood mixture and cook together for 3 to 5 minutes, until the shrimp are pink and curled and the scallops are opaque. Liquid should be cooked away, forming a flavorful glaze on the seafood and vegetables.

To make the fajitas, spoon about 1/3 cup of the seafood and vegetable mixture over a warm flour tortilla. Top with salsa or Pico de Gallo, cheese, tomatoes and sour cream. Fold tortillas like soft tacos and eat with your fingers. Have plenty of napkins handy.

Makes 8 servings.

Pico de Gallo

2 small, ripe tomatoes, seeded and
  chopped
2 fresh green jalapeno peppers,
  seeded and chopped
2 green onions, finely chopped
1 clove garlic, crushed through a press
2 tablespoons lemon juice
1 tablespoon olive oil
4 tablespoons fresh chopped cilantro
1/4 teaspoon salt
1/4 teaspoon ground cumin

Combine all ingredients in the bowl of a food processor or blender. Process briefly, long enough to make a chunky salsa. Do not puree. Allow flavors to blend before serving.

Makes 1 cup.

 Make the salsa up to 2 days in advance and store in the refrigerator.

ENTREES

Fish Facts

The Top 10 types of fish and seafood in the United States are tuna (mostly canned), shrimp, cod, Alaskan pollock (mostly consumed as imitation crab), salmon, catfish, flounder or sole, scallops and crab. Most seafood purveyors sell these year-round and carry other types of fish and seafood according to season and regional preferences.

Most types of fish and shellfish are more or less interchangeable, depending on the way in which they're cooked, according to the National Fisheries Institute. Here's a quick and handy guide:

Shellfish: This category is a hodgepodge of shellfish, mollusks and crustaceans including shrimp, scallops, clams, oysters, mussels, crab and conch. I also lump in a few marine critters, such as squid, that don't have shells but are cooked like shellfish.

Shellfish can be grilled, baked, microwaved, sauteed, deep-fried, poached or broiled. Many, such as clams, lobster, mussels and squid, are terrific in chowders, stews and soups because the meat doesn't fall apart.

They have enough flavor to stand up to very robust seasonings. Most shellfish, such as shrimp, scallops, mussels and squid, can be used in a range of Oriental, Mexican, Italian or French dishes. They're great with robust flavors such as blue cheese and garlic, and with mild flavors including spinach, butter, cream or sherry.

Often shellfish are removed from the shell, seasoned and returned to the shell for cooking and serving. The shell serves two functions: It protects the meat from overcooking and drying and it provides flavor.

Flaky fish: Flaky fish have a delicate texture and fall apart easily or separate into small flakes when cooked. The meat is mild and delicate in flavor.

Common members of the flaky fish category are cod, tilapia, haddock, flounder, orange roughy and pollock. Whiting, Pacific rockfish, any kind of sole, lake whitefish and kingklip also fall in this category.

Flaky, delicate fish are best sauteed, baked, deep-fried, microwaved, broiled or poached. Fillets of flaky fish also can be grilled on a barbecue if they are wrapped in aluminum foil or placed in a special, hinged fish-grilling rack. Fillets are excellent cooked en papillote (sealed in parchment paper or aluminum foil) or steamed inside banana leaves.

Most flaky fish aren't suited to cooking in chowders because the meat disintegrates in the liquid. Cod and red snapper can be used in soups and chowders if they aren't simmered too long.

Flaky fish taste best served with mild cream or butter sauces, dusted in seasoned bread crumbs or paired with mildly piquant flavors such as capers, tartar sauce, lemon juice or white wine. Spices and herbs should also be low-key to keep from overpowering the taste of the fish. Dill, basil, oregano, white pepper and tarragon are complementary flavors.

Medium-firm fish: Medium-firm fish have a close-knit texture that separates into large flakes or clumps when cooked. This category of versatile and extremely popular fish includes grouper, snapper, salmon, pompano, bluefish, amberjack, mackerel, mullet, mahi mahi, catfish and trout. Chub, sturgeon, walleye and sea bass are in this category also.

Most medium-firm fish are sold as fillets, often with the skin attached. Some species, such as salmon, also can be sold as steaks.

Medium-firm fish can be grilled, broiled, baked, microwaved, poached, sauteed or deep-fried. Several members of this category, including salmon, grouper and mahi mahi, are terrific in chowders and soups because they're hardy enough to stand up to simmering. Salmon, pompano, mahi mahi and catfish are also excellent en papillote.

Medium-firm fish such as salmon, mackerel, amberjack and bluefish tend to be high in natural fish oils. The oil gives them strong or distinctive flavors. They can stand up to an assortment of lively marinades and sauces. Cajun or blackening spices, garlic, onions, green onions, ginger, mustard and other strong seasonings go well with medium-firm fish.

Firm fish: Firm fish have a dense, meaty texture that doesn't flake or fall apart when cooked. Fresh tuna, swordfish, shark, marlin, halibut and monkfish belong in this category. The meat is sturdy enough that it can be cooked as steaks or fillets, or cubed and skewered for kebabs.

Firm fish can be grilled, broiled, baked, poached, stir-fried, sauteed, microwaved or deep-fried. The solid meat makes these fish perfect to add to stews, chowders and soups. Choose a flaky or medium-firm fish for dishes cooked en papillote.

With their meaty texture, these fish can stand up to almost any kind of sauce. The steaks can be marinated in teriyaki sauce, garlic, herbs and olive oil, wine or fruit juices.

Seasonings also can be robust and include ginger, curry, chili, Cajun spices, mint, fried onions, nuts or sesame seeds.

Quick reference for some fish and shellfish substitutions:

White meat with very light, delicate flavor and flaky, tender texture: (microwave, bake, poach, saute, steam, en papillote)

Cod	Pacific sand dab	Summer flounder
Cusk	Petrale sole	Tilefish
Dover sole	Rex sole	Witch flounder
Haddock	Southern flounder	Yellowtail flounder
Lake whitefish	Spotted cabrilla	Yellowtail snapper

White meat with a moderate flavor and flaky, tender texture: (microwave, bake, broil, poach, saute, steam, deep fry, en papillote)

American plaice (sea dab)	English sole	Sea trout
Arrowtooth flounder	Lingcod	Starry flounder
Butterfish	Pacific whiting	Whiting
Catfish	Rock sole	Winter flounder
Cobia	Sauger	Wolffish
	Snook	

Light meat, moderate flavor and moderately firm texture: (microwave, bake, grill, broil, poach, deep fry)

Alaskan pollock	Orange roughy	Walleye
Brook trout	Pacific ocean perch	White crappie
Giant sea bass	Rainbow trout	White king salmon
Grouper	Red snapper	White sea bass
Kingfish	Smelt	White sea trout
Mahi mahi	Tautog	

Darker meat, moderate flavor and moderately firm texture: (microwave, bake, grill, broil, saute, steam, poach, en papillote)

Amberjack	Jewfish	Pollock
Atlantic Ocean perch	King salmon (chinook)	Pompano
Atlantic salmon	Lake Chub	Rockfish
Black drum (kingfish)	Lake herring	Sable
Buffalofish	Lake sturgeon	Sculp (porgie)
Burbot	Lake trout	Sheepshead
Carp	Mangrove snapper	Silver salmon (coho)
Chum salmon	Monkfish	Spot
Crevalle jack	Mullet	Striped bass
Croaker	Northern pike	Vermillion snapper
Eel	Perch	
Greenland turbot	Pink salmon	

Dark meat, moderate flavor and firm texture: (grill, broil, microwave, saute, poach, steam, pickle, stew)

Atlantic mackerel	King mackerel	Sockeye salmon (red)
Black sea bass	Tuna (all varieties)	Spanish mackerel
Bluefish	Shark (all varieties)	Swordfish

Crabs: (microwave, steam, bake, saute)

Alaskan king crab   Jonah crab   Soft-shell crab
Blue crab   Red crab   Snow crab
Dungeness crab

Shrimp: (microwave, steam, saute, bake, grill, broil, poach, en papillote, stew, deep fry)

Blue shrimp   Key West shrimp   Rock shrimp
Brown shrimp   Northern shrimp   Tiger shrimp
California shrimp   Pink shrimp   White shrimp

Lobsters: (steam, saute, poach, bake, grill, broil, stew)

American lobster (Maine)
Rock lobster
Slipper lobster
Spiny lobster

Clams: (steam, bake, stew, grill, microwave, deep fry)

Butter clam   Hard clam (quahog)   Razor clam
Goeduck clam   Littleneck clam   Steamer clams

Mussels (microwave, stew, broil, bake, poach, saute)

Blue mussel
California mussel
Green lip mussel

Oysters: (microwave, stew, bake, broil, saute, poach, steam, deep fry)

Apalachicola oyster   Gulf oyster   Pacific oyster
Atlantic oyster   Olympia oyster   Soft American oyster

Scallops: (microwave, bake, broil, grill, deep fry, steam, poach, stew, saute)

Bay scallop
Calico scallop
Sea scallop

Mollusks: (bake, grill, deep fry, pickle, stew)

Abalone
Cockle
Conch
Welk

Cephalopods: (grill, poach, deep fry, saute, pickle, stew)

Octopus
Squid

(from the National Fisheries Institute)

This is an Oriental version of fish en papillote (paa-pee-YOHT), a French term for foods that are steam-baked in sealed packets. Citrus juices, fresh ginger, sesame oil, toasted, nutty sesame seeds and crisp snow peas star in this easy, elegant entree.

Seafood in Sesame Packets

6 sheets of parchment paper or aluminum foil
2 pounds skinless pompano fillets
1/4 pound snow peas, stems and strings removed
1 tablespoon fresh ginger, minced
2 tablespoons sesame seeds, toasted
2 tablespoons orange juice, preferably freshly squeezed with pulp
2 tablespoons lime juice, freshly squeezed
1 teaspoon Oriental sesame oil
2 tablespoons low-sodium soy sauce

orange roughy, grouper, snapper, perch, scallops, shelled shrimp, lobster tail

The packets can be filled and folded up to 8 hours in advance.

Notes: Parchment is a heavy, grease- and moisture-resistant paper that can be used in an oven. Professional bakers use it to line baking pans to prevent cookies, cakes and pastries from sticking. Parchment is available by the roll from specialty-food shops and in cake-decorating supply stores. Some bakeries sell parchment by the sheet.

Oriental sesame oil is made from toasted sesame seeds and has a distinct nutty aroma and flavor. It's used for flavoring, not for cooking or frying. Sesame oil is available in most grocery stores, health-food stores or Oriental markets.

Preheat oven to 425 F.

Cut the parchment paper into 6 rectangles measuring about 8 by 10 inches. Cut the fish into individual serving pieces, each weighing about 5 ounces. Place the fish near one end of the parchment, at least 1 inch from the edge of the paper.

Slice the snow peas lengthwise into thin strips. Top the fish fillets with a few sliced snow peas, a sprinkling of ginger and about 1/2 teaspoon of sesame seeds.

In a small container, mix the orange juice, lime juice, sesame oil and soy sauce. Spoon about 1 to 1 1/2 tablespoons of this mixture evenly over one piece of fish at a time.

Fold the parchment over to enclose the fish. Crimp the edges of the paper together to form a tight seal. Place the packets an inch apart on a jellyroll pan. Bake for 12 minutes and serve in the parchment or foil packets.

If using parchment, the packets may be cooked in a microwave oven. Place on a microwave-safe plate. Cook each packet individually on high (100 percent) power for 2 minutes and 10 seconds. Give fish a quarter turn and cook on high (100 percent) power for 30 seconds longer. Allow fish to stand 2 minutes before serving.

Excellent with rice or orzo and a vegetable.

Makes 6 servings.

The smoky flavor of the almonds and the bacon give this dish a real Southern flavor. Leftovers, if any, are terrific served cold.

Smokehouse-Almond Fish

1 pound fish fillets
2 strips bacon
3 ounces smoke-flavored almonds
    (1/2 of a 6-ounce can)
2 tablespoons cornmeal
1/4 teaspoon pepper
1 tablespoon lemon juice
2 tablespoons chopped fresh
    parsley
Lemon wedges

 catfish, grouper, cod, kingklip, orange roughy

In a non-stick skillet, fry the bacon until crisp. Crumble and set aside. Pour all but 2 tablespoons of grease from the pan and set aside.

Place the almonds, cornmeal and pepper in the bowl of a food processor or blender. Grind the nuts until they are very fine. Place the nuts in a shallow bowl or a pie plate. Dredge the fish fillets in the almond meal to make a thick coating.

Heat the bacon grease in the non-stick skillet and fry the fillets over medium-low heat. Cook for 7 minutes and turn carefully. Add remaining nut mixture to the pan. Cook the fish for 5 to 6 minutes longer, depending on thickness. Watch carefully to prevent nuts from burning.

Drizzle lemon juice over fish and stir to moisten nuts. Transfer to plates and top with crumbled bacon and chopped parsley. Serve with lemon wedges.

Makes 4 serving.

Note: If the nuts start to burn before the fish fillets are thoroughly cooked, transfer to a microwave-safe dish and cook on high (100 percent) power for 1 to 2 minutes.

This is a memorable combination of fish, fruit and spices. The topping is a sweet-savory apple and pear relish that takes about 10 minutes to make.

Spice-Rubbed Salmon with Apple-Pear Relish

1 3/4 to 2 pounds salmon fillets, skin and bones removed
Spice Rub (recipe follows)
1 1/2 tablespoons canola or olive oil, divided in half
1/3 cup onion, finely diced (1 small onion)
1 Red Bartlett pear, unpeeled and cut into bite-sized chunks
1 apple, peeled and cut into bite-size chunks
3 tablespoons red bell pepper, finely minced (about 1/4 of a red pepper)
2 tablespoons brown sugar
1/4 cup white-wine vinegar
1/4 cup dry sherry or apple juice
1 tablespoon lemon juice
1/8 teaspoon salt
1/8 teaspoon white pepper

Preheat oven to 425 F.

Rinse salmon under cold water. Pat dry. Leave whole or cut into four serving pieces. Rub fillet with 1/2 tablespoon of the canola or olive oil and dredge in the Spice Rub. Refrigerate fish in a glass or ceramic baking dish while making the Apple-Pear Relish.

To make the sauce, heat the remaining oil in a non-stick skillet. Saute the onion for 1 minute, then add the pear, apple and pepper. Cook over medium heat, stirring frequently, until the fruit softens. Add the brown sugar, vinegar, sherry or apple juice, lemon juice, salt and white pepper. Cook for 5 minutes longer, until the liquid begins to evaporate and the fruit develops a glazed appearance. Don't allow the fruit to cook dry or fall apart. If desired, relish can be prepared in advance and reheated while the salmon is cooking.

Bake the salmon for 14 to 16 minutes, until the fish is firm and the spice mixture is dark brown. Divide into portions and serve with 1/4 cup to 1/3 cup of the Apple-Pear Relish.

Makes 4 to 6 servings.

Note: The salmon can also be sauteed over medium heat in a non-stick skillet for 5 to 6 minutes per side. It can also be cooked in a microwave oven. Cover the fish with waxed paper and cook on high (100 percent) power for 3 minutes. Turn the dish and cook 3 minutes longer.

Spice Rub

2 tablespoons curry powder
1 tablespoon cumin powder
1 teaspoon sugar
1/2 teaspoon salt
1/2 teaspoon paprika
1/4 teaspoon cardamom

Combine curry powder, cumin powder, sugar, salt, paprika and cardamom. Place in a shallow plate and use to dredge fish. Makes 1/4 cup.

How to select fish:

• Look for bright, shiny fillets. They should be firm to the touch.

• Buy from a reputable source such as a grocery store or established seafood market.

• Smell the fish; it should smell faintly of the sea. It shouldn't smell "fishy" or like ammonia. The store should also smell fresh and clean.

• Be flexible; if you can't find the particular type of fish you're looking for, ask about alternatives.

• Avoid fillets and steaks that show signs of bruises or blood spots.

• Avoid any fish that is filmy or sitting in fluid.

• Frozen fish may be better quality than old "fresh" fish. Look for packages without frost buildup or signs of dryness or freezer burn (the flesh will look white and opaque). Look for individually wrapped fillets.

• Buy frozen fish if you don't plan on eating it within two days.

• Whole fish can be stored directly on ice because the skin keeps it from absorbing water. Fillets and steaks should be protected from direct contact with ice so they don't become water-logged.

• Many kinds of fish, such as tuna, are very dark when raw but become lighter when cooked. Swordfish has natural striations of color that don't affect the flavor.

Louise Wainwright Simpson, my dear friend from Phoenix, Arizona, gave me this terrific recipe. Trout has a sweet, almost nutty flavor that is highlighted by the walnuts and chutney.

Trout with Chutney and Walnuts

4 trout fillets (about 1/2 pound)
4 tablespoons milk
2 tablespoons flour
1/2 teaspoon salt
1/4 teaspoon white pepper
1 tablespoon butter
1 tablespoon oil
3 tablespoons lemon juice
8 tablespoons mango chutney or other fruit chutney
4 tablespoons toasted chopped walnuts

catfish, monkfish, orange roughy, pompano, sea trout

Dust the fish in the flour up to 30 minutes in advance and store between sheets of wax paper in the refrigerator.

In a shallow plate, combine the flour, salt and pepper. Dip the fish in the milk and dredge it in the seasoned flour.

Heat the butter and oil in a large non-stick skillet. When the butter starts to foam, fry the fillets skin-side down for 4 minutes, until the flour coating is crisp. Turn carefully and fry on other side for 4 minutes. Transfer to warmed plates.

Pour the lemon juice in the pan and stir to include any brown bits from the frying. Stir in the chutney and walnuts. Bring to a boil, remove from heat and spoon about 3 tablespoons of the mixture over each trout fillet.

Makes 4 servings.

Note: Trout is a fish that freezes very well. Farm-raised trout is excellent quality with ivory-colored flesh and very few bones.

Every summer when I was growing up, my father fly-cast for trout in the cold, clear springs of Colorado and New Mexico. He was a good fisherman and the only part of his catch I didn't enjoy was eating around all those fine fish bones. Now, farm-raised trout is available already cut into fillets and practically bone-free.

Trout Amandine

2 trout fillets
3 tablespoons flour
1/4 teaspoon salt
1/8 teaspoon pepper
2 tablespoons unsalted butter
1 tablespoon olive oil
1/4 cup sliced almonds
1 tablespoon lemon juice
2 tablespoons chopped fresh parsley

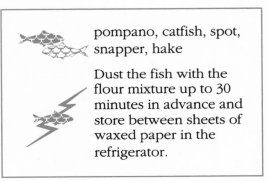

pompano, catfish, spot, snapper, hake

Dust the fish with the flour mixture up to 30 minutes in advance and store between sheets of waxed paper in the refrigerator.

Mix the flour with the salt and pepper. Dredge the trout fillets in the mixture and shake off any excess flour.

Heat the butter and olive oil in a non-stick skillet over medium-high heat. When butter starts to foam, add the trout fillets, skin-side down. Saute about 5 minutes, until the skin is golden brown. Use a spatula to carefully turn the fish. Lower heat to keep butter and oil from burning. Cook 3 to 4 minutes longer. Transfer fish to individual plates.

Add the almonds to the skillet and fry about 3 minutes until slightly browned. Stir in the lemon juice and parsley. Spoon the almonds and parsley and a little of the butter over each fillet.

Makes 2 servings.

Note: This recipe can be doubled. Cook the fish in two batches. Be careful not to overcook!

This is an unlikely sounding combination but it's excellent, especially in the first cool days of fall. The nutty flavor of trout finds a soulmate in the nutty legumes. French cooks often combine the two. Serve with De Loach Sonoma County chardonnay or pinot noir.

Trout on a Bed
of Lentils with Sherry Vinaigrette

4 trout fillets
1 tablespoon honey
1 tablespoon red wine vinegar
1/4 teaspoon black pepper or lemon
   pepper
1 cup dry lentils
3 cups water
1 bay leaf
1 teaspoon salt
1/2 teaspoon thyme leaves
1/4 cup dry sherry
2 tablespoons red wine vinegar
3 tablespoons olive oil
1 green onion, finely chopped

salmon, mackerel

Cook the lentils up to 4 days in advance and reheat in a microwave oven while broiling the fish.

In a microwave-safe measuring cup, combine the honey, black pepper and 1 tablespoon red wine vinegar. Heat on high (100 percent) power, until boiling. Arrange fish in an oven-proof baking dish. Drizzle honey and vinegar mixture evenly over the fish. Refrigerate until ready to cook.

Wash the lentils and place in a sauce pan; add the water, bay leaf, salt and thyme leaves. Bring to a boil and cook uncovered for 15 minutes or until the water has almost evaporated. Lentils should be tender but not mushy. Pour off cooking liquid and discard bay leaf.

Pour the sherry over the lentils and cook for 4 to 5 minutes longer until the sherry cooks away. Remove from heat and pour 2 tablespoons red wine vinegar and olive oil over lentils. Stir in chopped green onion. Cover and set aside while broiling trout. Heat the oven broiler. Cook the fish about 4 inches from the broiler for 4 to 5 minutes until opaque and firm to the touch. Spoon the lentils onto a serving plate and arrange the trout fillets on top. Serve warm.

Makes 4 servings.

Note: You can cook the lentils in a microwave oven: Combine lentils, water, bay leaf, thyme leaves and salt. Cover and cook for 14 minutes on high (100 percent) until tender. Allow to stand in cooking liquid for 5 minutes. Drain. Add sherry, red wine vinegar, olive oil and green onion and cook for 5 minutes on high (100 percent) power.

With good ingredients, you can't help but have a good dish. Canned hearts of palm are available in most grocery stores and sun-dried tomatoes are becoming more common as well. You can buy parchment by the sheet from a bakery or a cake decorating store or you can substitute aluminum foil.

Fish, Hearts of Palm and Sun-Dried Tomatoes en Papillote

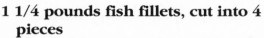

1 1/4 pounds fish fillets, cut into 4 pieces
8 sun-dried tomatoes, marinated in oil
2 hearts of palm, sliced crosswise into 8 medallions
1 teaspoon thyme leaves
Salt and pepper
4 (12-inch) pieces parchment paper, cut into heart shapes

pompano, trout, orange roughy, flounder, sole, mackerel, snapper, grouper, tuna, mahi mahi

Coarsely chop the sun-dried tomatoes. Arrange each fillet on a sheet of parchment paper. Top with sun-dried tomatoes, slices of hearts of palm and thyme. Sprinkle lightly with salt and pepper. Starting at the pointed end, fold the edges of the paper tightly to form a good seal.

(You may also use a square piece of paper and gather the ends in a purse. Twist the top firmly to seal. Tie with string or ribbon.)

Place the packets in a circle on a plate or in the corners of a 2-quart, microwave-safe baking dish. Leave the center clear. Cook on high (100 percent) power for 5 minutes. Turn dish and cook on high for 2 minutes longer. Allow packets to stand for 2 to 3 minutes before opening.

Makes 4 servings.

Note: Dried, non-marinated tomatoes can substitute in this recipe. Soak the tomatoes in warm water for 5 minutes to soften. Drain and chop into pieces. Toss the pieces with 1 tablespoon olive oil.

Cooking the fish in milk sweetens it and mellows the garlic. This dish is a very delicious surprise.

Garlic Poached Fish

2 pounds fish fillets
1 cup low-fat milk
4 cloves of garlic, crushed through a press
1/2 teaspoon paprika
1/4 teaspoon salt
1/4 teaspoon sugar
Pinch nutmeg
2 teaspoons butter
1 tablespoon flour

 sole, turbot, orange roughy, cod, perch, butterfish, snapper, halibut, pompano

In a 1-quart, microwave-safe baking dish, combine the milk, garlic, salt, paprika, sugar and nutmeg. Cover and cook on high (100 percent) power until the milk comes to a boil. Add the fillets to the milk, with thick parts toward the outside and thin parts toward the center. If fillets aren't covered by the liquid, spoon some over the fish. Cover and cook on high (100 percent) power for 3 minutes. Give dish a one-quarter turn and cook for 3 to 4 minutes longer. Allow to stand 1 minute.

Use a flat spatula to remove fish to warm plates or a serving platter. Reserve the cooking liquid.

In a small dish, mash the butter and the flour together to form a lump. Stir this into the cooking liquid, until the butter melts. Cook on high (100 percent) power for 1 minute. Stir and cook until liquid is boiling and thickened. Pour sauce over fish.

Makes 5 servings.

Note: This is a good dish to serve with spinach or tomato pasta. The pale pink sauce is a nice contrast to the colored pasta.

By cooking the fish on medium (50 percent) power in a microwave oven, it cooks more evenly and exudes more flavorful juices. It also prevents the fish from popping.

Fillets with a Chutney Glaze

1 3/4 pounds fish fillets
1/4 teaspoon salt
1/4 teaspoon pepper
1 cup good-quality chutney
1 tablespoon lemon juice
1 tablespoon soy sauce

 orange roughy, cod, snapper, grouper, tuna, salmon, pompano, scallops, shrimp

Arrange the fillets in a microwave-safe baking dish with the thick portions toward the outside and thin portions toward the center. Tuck any very thin pieces underneath to ensure even cooking. Sprinkle with salt and pepper.

In a small bowl, combine the chutney, lemon juice and soy sauce. Stir and pour evenly over the fillets. Cover with wax paper. Cook on medium (50 percent) power for 4 minutes. Turn dish and cook on medium (50 percent) power for 4 minutes longer. Spoon some of the sauce over the fish. Cover and cook on high (100 percent) power for 1 minute longer. Allow to stand 2 to 3 minutes before removing from dish.

Makes 4 servings.

Note: This is also excellent with Mango Salsa (recipe page 198) instead of the Chutney Glaze.

The term provencal (proh-vahn-SAHL) means the dish is flavored with the signature ingredients of the Provence region of Southern France, namely tomatoes, capers, garlic and olive oil. Monkfish is traditional in Provence where it's called lotte or baudroie.

Monkfish Provencal

1 1/4 pounds monkfish fillets
2 tablespoons olive oil, divided
2 shallots, peeled and minced or 1
**   small yellow onion**
2 cloves garlic, crushed through a
**   press**
1 ripe tomato (about 8 ounces)
2 teaspoons capers, drained
1/2 teaspoon thyme leaves
1/4 teaspoon salt
1/4 teaspoon black pepper
2 tablespoons chopped fresh parsley

 mahi mahi, grouper, snapper, sea bass, kingfish, shark, mackerel, bluefish

Place 1 tablespoon of the olive oil in a microwave-safe baking dish. Coat the fillets with the oil and arrange in spokes with thick parts toward the outside and thin portions toward the center of the dish.

Slice the tomato in half around the middle and squeeze gently to remove the seeds and juice. Chop finely. Combine with the remaining olive oil, shallots, garlic, capers, thyme leaves, salt, pepper and parsley. Sprinkle over fish.

Cover and cook on medium (50 percent) power for 10 to 12 minutes, turning dish once halfway through the cooking. Fish is done when it is firm to the touch. Allow to stand 1 minute.

Divide fish into serving pieces. Serve with bread or rice.

Makes 4 servings.

Notes: During the summer, a good alternative is to cook the fish as directed with just the shallots and garlic. Mix the tomato with the remaining ingredients and serve those as a cool topping with the warm fish. For a similar recipe, see Spanish-Style Grilled Fish with Olive and Pimento Relish (recipe page 59).

The dish can also be baked at 400 F in a conventional oven. Oil the baking dish and arrange fillets in a single layer. In a non-stick skillet, heat remaining oil and saute the shallots, garlic and tomato. Stir in the thyme leaves and capers and cook for 3 to 4 minutes. Pour the tomato mixture over the fish. Bake uncovered for 12 to 15 minutes, or until fish is firm and opaque.

Neville Cutting, a good friend and the owner of Cutting Loose, a world-class fishing expedition company based in Winter Park, guides salmon trips to Alaska several times a year. This showy party dish is his favorite no-fail recipe and it's about as easy as cooking gets. Use very fresh fish. Serve it on Thanksgiving and forget the turkey.

Whole Steamed Salmon in Foil

1 5- to 8-pound silver salmon, head on
   if desired
1/2 lemon
1 carrot, peeled
1 small onion, peeled
1 stalk celery
1/2 teaspoon fines herbs or other
   herb blend
Salt and pepper to taste
1 (6-ounce) box chicken-flavored
   stuffing mix
1/4 cup white wine
2 tablespoons oil or non-stick olive oil
   cooking spray

 snapper, grouper, bluefish, sea bass

Notes: The best match for this is Louise Cutting's Tarragon Cream Sauce (recipe page 199). During the summer, cook the fish on a barbecue grill over medium heat. Turn the fish once halfway through cooking, taking care not to puncture the foil.

Have the fish seller remove the scales and gills from the fish. Squeeze the lemon juice in the cavity.

Preheat oven to 450 F. In the bowl of a food processor or blender, chop the carrot, onion and celery. Combine it with the herbs, salt and pepper and stuffing. Barely moisten with the white wine; the stuffing should be fairly dry.

Fill the cavity of the fish with stuffing. Measure the fish at the thickest part. Fish will need 10 minutes for every inch of thickness, plus 10 minutes for the stuffing.

(For example, a fish that measures 3 inches will require 40 minutes of baking time. A fish that measures 3 1/2 inches will require 45 minutes.)

Brush a large sheet of aluminum foil with the oil or spray fish with non-stick olive oil cooking spray. Wrap the fish well in several layers of foil. Bake for required time.

Open foil and test fish for doneness by inserting a wooden skewer in the thickest part. The skewer should slide in without resistance. Allow the fish to rest 5 minutes. Peel away the foil; the skin on the underside should come off with it.

Use a spoon to scrape out the stuffing. Carefully, transfer the fish to a platter and remove the skin on top using a sharp knife. It will peel off easily; discard.

Garnish with parsley and lemon slices. If the head is on the fish, place a lemon slice over the eye.

Makes 8 to 10 servings, depending on size of fish.

People get nervous just seeing the word "anchovy," but in this dish, a dab of anchovy paste adds saltiness and flavor without overpowering the sauce.

Fish Steaks
in a Mellow Anchovy-Tomato Sauce

1 1/4 pounds fish steaks or thick fillets
1 tablespoon olive oil
2 shallots, finely chopped or 1/4 cup chopped yellow onion
1 tablespoon lemon juice
1 1/2 teaspoons anchovy paste
2 tablespoons tomato paste
1/3 cup whipping cream
Minced fresh parsley

 halibut, monkfish, red snapper, perch, mahi mahi, orange roughy, sea trout

In a 2-quart, microwave-safe baking dish, combine the olive oil and shallots. Cook on high (100 percent) power for 1 1/2 minutes. Stir. Place the fish in the dish and flip over to coat both sides evenly with the oil and shallots. (Place so thicker parts are toward the outside and thin parts are toward the center of the dish.)

In a measuring cup, stir together the lemon juice, anchovy paste, tomato paste and whipping cream. Pour over fish. Cover with waxed paper. Cook on high (100 percent) power for 5 minutes. Give dish a one-quarter turn. Cook on high (100 percent) power for 1 to 2 minutes longer. If the meat feels firm to the touch, remove dish and allow to stand 2 minutes before serving. Garnish with parsley.

Makes 4 servings.

Note: Imported anchovy paste is available in tubes similar to toothpaste. Squeeze out what you need and keep the rest stored in the refrigerator.

In Naples, "alla pizzaiola" meant meat, chicken or fish baked in a rich tomato sauce with the flavors of a pizza. Use any of the good commercial spaghetti sauces available in the grocery store and dress it up with a little extra garlic, oregano and mushrooms. This makes a fast, beautiful dinner.

Pesce Pizzaiola

1 pound red snapper
1 1/2 cups mushroom-flavored
　spaghetti sauce
4 ounces sliced mushrooms
1 clove garlic, crushed through a press
1/2 teaspoon oregano
4 ounces shredded part-skim
　mozzarella cheese
1 tablespoon grated Parmesan cheese

orange roughy, catfish fillets,
mahi mahi, tuna, perch,
monkfish

Preheat oven to 425 F.

Lightly coat a baking dish with non-stick cooking spray. Arrange the fish in the baking dish, tucking any thin edges under. Sprinkle fish with the mushrooms. Stir together the spaghetti sauce, garlic and oregano. Pour over the fish. Sprinkle the mozzarella cheese on top and sprinkle surface with Parmesan cheese. Bake for 10 minutes. Turn oven to broil. Cook fish under broiler for 2 to 3 minutes longer, until cheese is bubbly and brown.

Remove from heat and allow to stand about 3 minutes before serving.

Makes 4 servings.

Notes: You can substitute a 4-ounce can or jar of mushroom stems and pieces for fresh sliced mushrooms if you wish. You can also vary the flavor using your favorite pizza toppings, including green or red peppers, onions or a few pieces of chopped pepperoni.

To prepare this dish in a microwave oven, place fish in a microwave-safe baking dish with the thin portions toward the center. Top with mushrooms and spaghetti sauce. Cover and cook on high (100 percent) power for 3 minutes. Rotate dish and cook for 2 minutes longer. Sprinkle with mozzarella and Parmesan cheeses. Cook for 1 minute longer and allow to stand at room temperature for 2 minutes before serving.

Top fish with a creamy cheese sauce and a few bright spears of broccoli and you can't go wrong. First-time fish eaters will flip for this one. It was inspired by the old standby, chicken divan.

Baked Fish with Broccoli and Two Cheeses

1 pound flaky fish such as flounder
1 (11-ounce) can condensed Cheddar cheese soup
1/3 cup low-fat milk
2 tablespoons white wine or vermouth
Pinch cayenne pepper
1 (10-ounce) package frozen broccoli spears, thawed and drained
1/4 cup grated Parmesan cheese

 perch, sole, orange roughy, cod, kingklip, haddock, catfish

Preheat oven to 425 F. Lightly coat a 9-by-9-inch baking dish with non-stick cooking spray.

Pat the fish fillets dry with a paper towel and arrange in the dish. Top each fillet with a few spears of broccoli.

In a small bowl, combine the soup, milk, wine and cayenne pepper. Mix well and pour over fish and broccoli. Sprinkle the Parmesan cheese over all. Bake for 12 minutes, until sauce is bubbling and fish is opaque. Serve hot.

Makes 4 servings.

Notes: To prepare this in a microwave oven, proceed as directed but cover with vented plastic wrap and cook on high (100 percent) power for 5 minutes. Rotate dish and cook on high (100 percent) power for 3 minutes longer. Allow to stand 3 minutes before serving.

Banquet Chef Doug Davis gave me the idea for this recipe when he worked for the Marriott Orlando World Center.

Tuscan-Style Fish in Parmesan Crust

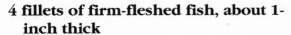

4 fillets of firm-fleshed fish, about 1-inch thick
1 egg
1 tablespoon water
4 tablespoons all-purpose flour
1/2 teaspoon oregano
1/2 teaspoon basil
1/4 teaspoon thyme leaves
1/4 teaspoon salt
1/8 teaspoon black pepper
4 tablespoons freshly grated Parmesan cheese
3 tablespoons olive oil

 snapper, grouper, catfish, monkfish, shark

In a shallow dish, whisk together the egg and 1 tablespoon of water. Set aside.

In another shallow dish or on a plate, mix together the flour, oregano, basil, thyme, salt and pepper.

Place the Parmesan cheese on a separate plate. Dip the fish fillets first in the flour mixture and shake away excess. Dip in the egg-water mixture and then in the Parmesan cheese. Set aside on waxed paper until all fillets are done. For a heavier coating, dip a second time in the Parmesan cheese mixture.

Heat the olive oil in a heavy, non-stick skillet over medium heat. It's important to cook this fish slowly to prevent the cheese from burning. Add the fillets and cook without crowding, about 5 minutes per side. Turn carefully with a spatula to avoid breaking the fillets.

Remove to warm plates and serve with lemon slices.

Makes 4 servings.

This wonderful dish looks fancy but it's a snap to make. The ingredients are simple, flavorful and inexpensive.

Fish Roll-Ups with Shrimp Stuffing

6 fish fillets (about 1 1/4 pounds)
8 medium shrimp
3 tablespoons butter
1 small onion, chopped (about 1/4 cup)
2 stalks celery heart, chopped (about 1/2 cup)
8 small mushrooms, chopped (about 1/2 cup)
2 cups soft bread crumbs
1/2 teaspoon salt
1/4 teaspoon pepper
1/2 teaspoon dried tarragon or marjoram or 2 tablespoons chopped fresh herbs

perch, orange roughy, flounder, sole, catfish

Preheat oven to 400 F. Coat a baking dish lightly with non-stick cooking spray.

Shell the shrimp, chop coarsely and set aside.

In a large, non-stick skillet, melt the butter over medium-high heat and saute the onion, celery and mushrooms for 5 minutes. You can also cook the vegetables on high (100 percent) power in a microwave oven for 3 minutes.

Stir in the bread crumbs, chopped shrimp, salt, pepper and tarragon or marjoram. Mix well to distribute butter among crumbs. If mixture is too dry, moisten with a little water or an additional tablespoon melted butter. Don't make the filling soggy because shrimp and fish will exude moisture during cooking.

Roll each fish fillet around a portion of the stuffing. Place seam-side down in the prepared baking dish. Sprinkle a little extra stuffing on top.

Bake for 20 to 25 minutes, or until stuffing on top is golden and fish is opaque. Serve with a wedge of lemon on each portion.

Makes 6 servings.

This is a perfect recipe for people who object to a "fishy" taste or smell. The creamy, mild Gorgonzola cheese in the sauce is the perfect foil for previously frozen fish. It's also great when made separately and poured over grilled fish. True Gorgonzola is made in a little town outside of Milan, Italy, and it has a savory flavor similar to blue cheese.

Fish with Gorgonzola Sauce

1 1/2 pounds fish fillets or steaks
1 tablespoon butter
1 tablespoon flour
1/4 teaspoon salt
1/4 teaspoon pepper
1/4 teaspoon nutmeg
1 cup evaporated skim milk
3 to 4 ounces Gorgonzola or other blue-style cheese, crumbled
2 tablespoons chopped fresh parsley for garnish

 halibut, grouper, sole, sea bass, haddock, snapper, perch

Arrange the fish fillets in a microwave-safe baking dish, with thickest parts of fillets toward the outside of the dish. Fold any very thin fillets over to cook more evenly. Set aside while preparing sauce.

In a separate microwave-safe dish, melt the butter on high (100 percent) power. Stir in the flour, salt, pepper and nutmeg and cook on high (100 percent) power for 30 seconds. Stir in the evaporated skim milk and cook on high (100 percent) power 1 to 2 minutes longer. Stir again and cook for 1 minute longer until milk is boiling and mixture has thickened. Stir in the Gorgonzola or other blue cheese until it partially melts.

Pour the sauce over the fish fillets. Do not cover. Cook on high (100 percent) power for 3 minutes. Rotate dish and cook another 3 to 4 minutes on high. Allow to stand two minutes at room temperature. Sprinkle with parsley before serving.

Makes 6 servings.

Note: You can also brown the surface by broiling it under the oven broiler for 1 to 2 minutes. To avoid overcooking the fish, subtract 1 minute from microwave cooking time.

This is a terrific starter recipe to try out on timid fish eaters. The sweet-savory flavor of the sauce is perfect for kids, too.

Baked Fish with Honey Mustard

1 1/4 pounds fish fillets
2 teaspoons olive oil
1 teaspoon lemon juice
3 tablespoons honey
3 tablespoons whole-grain mustard
1/8 teaspoon paprika
1 tablespoon mayonnaise

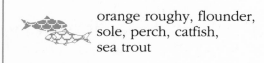
orange roughy, flounder, sole, perch, catfish, sea trout

Preheat the oven to 400 F.

Coat a baking dish with non-stick cooking spray. Arrange the fillets in the dish and fold any thin edges under so each fillet is an even thickness.

In a small dish, combine the olive oil, lemon juice, honey, mustard, paprika and mayonnaise. Pour over fish. Bake for 10 minutes or longer if fillets are very thick. Turn on the oven broiler. Broil for 2 minutes, or until the sauce is brown and lightly blistered on top.

Stir sauce to prevent separation and serve hot.

Makes 4 servings.

Lemon Poached Fish on Wild Rice

1 pound flaky fish fillets
1 box wild and white rice mix
1 cup water
2 tablespoons lemon juice
2 chicken-flavor bouillon cubes
1/2 cup green onions, sliced on the
    diagonal
1/4 teaspoon thyme leaves
1/4 teaspoon white pepper
1/2 cup carrots, thinly sliced on the
    diagonal
Paprika for garnish

 snapper, cod, orange roughy, perch, halibut, haddock, turbot, flounder, sole

Prepare the wild and white rice according to the package instructions.

While the rice is cooking, combine the water, lemon juice, bouillon cubes, green onions, thyme and pepper in a deep skillet. Bring liquid to a boil. Cover and simmer 5 minutes. Add the carrot and simmer 3 to 4 minutes longer. Reduce the heat until the mixture is simmering. Lay the fish fillets in the liquid without crowding. Cover and simmer for 9 to 10 minutes, until the fish is opaque and flakes easily.

Divide rice between individual plates. Arrange one fillet and some of the vegetables on the rice. Spoon the poaching liquid over all. (If the mixture is too soupy, remove all the fish and vegetables from the pan, then boil the remaining liquid until it has reduced slightly.) Pour liquid over the fish and rice. Garnish with paprika.

Makes 4 servings.

Couscous, a delicious granular pasta from Morocco, combines with herbs to make a flavorful breading. You can assemble this dish in the morning and cook it at night.

Herb and Couscous Crusted Fish

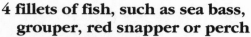

4 fillets of fish, such as sea bass, grouper, red snapper or perch
1/2 cup couscous
1/2 teaspoon salt
1 1/4 cups boiling water
1/2 bunch parsley, minced
2 teaspoons crushed dried marjoram
1/2 teaspoon thyme leaves
1/2 teaspoon dried basil
2 1/2 tablespoons melted butter or margarine
1/4 teaspoon black pepper

perch, sea bass, grouper, snapper, catfish, pompano, shark

Preheat oven to 400 F.

Rinse fish under cold running water and pat dry with paper towels.

Combine the couscous and salt in a mixing bowl. Pour the boiling water over and allow to stand 15 minutes until the water has been absorbed. Toss with a fork.

Add the parsley, marjoram, thyme and basil to the mixing bowl. Stir in the melted butter and pepper. Spread mixture over each fillet; pat to make it adhere to the surface.

Coat a 2-quart baking dish lightly with non-stick cooking spray. Add the fish and bake for 12 minutes. Turn on oven broiler and brown the top of the fish for 2 to 4 minutes longer.

Serve hot.

Makes 4 servings.

Notes: To make this dish more than a day in advance, make the couscous coating and refrigerate tightly covered. When ready to cook, coat and bake the fish.

The delicate pink meat and the green pastel sauce make this dish as beautiful as it is delicious. To save time, partially make the broccoli sauce in advance. The sauce is also excellent over shellfish, such as scallops or shrimp.

Poached Salmon in Broccoli Sauce

2 cups water
1 cup white wine
2 teaspoons white wine vinegar
1 stalk celery, cut into 1-inch cubes
2 green onions, cut into 1-inch cubes
3 peppercorns or 1/4 teaspoon
　　ground black pepper
1/2 teaspoon salt
1 1/2 to 2 pounds salmon fillets or
　　steaks

 halibut, trout, striped bass

Combine the water, wine, vinegar and remaining ingredients except salmon in a large saucepan, kettle or fish poacher. Bring to a boil and boil for 10 minutes.

Check salmon for bones by running your fingers along the fillet. Use tweezers to pull out the bones.

Reduce the heat under the poaching liquid until it simmers. Place the fish, skin-side down, in the poaching liquid. Do not allow it to boil. Cook for 6 minutes. Turn off the heat and allow the fish to stand in the liquid for 4 to 5 minutes longer.

Use a large, slotted spatula to remove the fillets. Place on a platter and peel away the skin and any bones. Discard and keep the fish warm.

Strain the liquid and reserve 2 cups of liquid for Broccoli Sauce (recipe follows).

Makes 6 servings.

Broccoli Sauce

1 bunch broccoli
1 tablespoon flour
1 tablespoon butter
2 cups reserved poaching liquid
1 teaspoon lemon juice

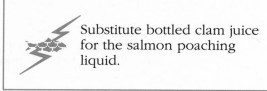 Substitute bottled clam juice for the salmon poaching liquid.

Trim the broccoli and remove the tender green florets. Reserve for another use.

Chop the stems coarsely. Add the stems to the poaching liquid and boil for 10 to 12 minutes. The broccoli should be very tender. Reserve the cooking water and puree the broccoli in a blender or food processor until very fine.

Melt the butter in a saucepan. Whisk in the flour and cook for 1 minute, until the flour is bubbling and golden. Gradually whisk in the reserved poaching liquid and broccoli puree. Stir in the lemon juice and bring mixture to a gentle boil. Thin with milk or cream if necessary.

Serve warm over poached salmon. If desired, cook the reserved broccoli florets and serve them on the side with the fish.

Makes 6 servings.

Know your fish

• Drawn: Whole fish minus internal organs. Has scales and gills. Trout and salmon are often sold this way. Buy 12 ounces per person.

• Dressed: Organs, scales, head, tail and fins removed. Dressed fish are ready to bake, steam, poach or grill. Use a hinged grill basket for grilling. Buy 8 ounces per person.

• Steaks: Slices cut crosswise from a large, dressed fish. Steaks are ready to cook, bake, broil or grill. Buy 4 to 6 ounces per person.

• Fillets: Boneless (or mostly boneless) pieces cut lengthwise from the sides of a fish. Most fillets are ready to bake, broil, fry, poach, steam or roll around a stuffing. Some fillets, such as salmon and mahi mahi are sold with the skin on. Buy 4 to 6 ounces per person.

• Frozen portions: Pieces cut from a fish and sold frozen. Thaw overnight in the refrigerator and cook as you would fresh fish. Buy 4 to 6 ounces per person.

Timing:

• Fish cooks more quickly than chicken or beef.

• Use the 10-minute rule: Cook fish for 10 minutes per inch of thickness. Measure the fish at the thickest point before cooking. A fillet that is 1 inch thick will cook in 10 minutes. A steak that is 2 inches thick will cook in 20 minutes.

• The 10-minute rule does not apply to cooking in the microwave oven. Cook 2 to 4 minutes on high (100 percent) power for each pound of fish. Or use the times listed in each recipe as guidelines. Increase cooking times for low-wattage microwave ovens.

• Check fish often because overcooking results in dry, flavorless meat.

• Fish is done when it is firm to the touch. Use your fingertips to press on the meat at the thickest part. If the meat feels spongy and soft, it needs to cook a little longer. If it feels firm, it's cooked. Be careful not to burn your fingers.

• Fish is done when the meat is opaque. If you prefer not to use your fingers, pierce the meat with a fork. Poke the tines into the thickest portion of the fish at a 45-degree angle and twist gently to pull up flakes of the fish. It should flake easily.

• Some fish, such as pike, cod, kingklip and perch flake very easily; others, such as mahi mahi, salmon and shark don't.

Run Down is a traditional Jamaican and Caribbean dish made with salt cod, coconut milk, onions, tomatoes and hot peppers. This fast and simple version uses fresh fish and canned coconut milk. The dish is often served with Mashed Plantains. Plantains are members of the banana family but their flesh is starchy and not as sweet.

Modern Jamaican Run Down

1 pound skinless fillets
1 cup fresh or canned coconut milk
1/2 cup water
1/4 teaspoon dried thyme leaves, or
  1/2 teaspoon fresh thyme chopped
1 medium yellow onion, chopped
2 tomatoes, seeded and chopped
1 clove garlic, minced
1 whole Scotch bonnet pepper
1 tablespoon malt or cider vinegar
1/2 teaspoon salt
1 green onion, chopped

 kingfish, grouper, tuna, mackerel, mahi mahi

Notes: The fish can also be cooked covered with the sauce in a microwave oven on high (100 percent) power for 6 minutes, or until firm. The sauce can be made and spooned over grilled fish. The fish should cook in about 12 to 15 minutes on a medium-hot grill.

Scotch bonnet peppers, also called habaneros, are extremely hot. They provide a sweet flavor as well as spice to many Jamaican dishes. To get the flavor without making the dish unbearably spicy, cook the pepper whole and do not allow the pepper to burst. For slightly more spice, add a few slivers of the pepper to the sauce and emulsify it in a blender. If Scotch bonnet peppers are unavailable, substitute jalapeno, serrano or Thai peppers.

The sauce can be made up to three days in advance and reheated immediately before cooking the fish.

Cut the fish into serving pieces and refrigerate until ready to cook.

In a shallow, non-stick skillet, combine coconut milk, onion, garlic, water, tomatoes, thyme and Scotch bonnet pepper. Bring to a boil. Reduce heat to a simmer and cook for 15 to 18 minutes, until coconut milk has reduced, turned a pale salmon color and is thick. Discard pepper.

Remove the mixture from heat and pour into a blender. Puree until smooth. The mixture should be pale pink. Return to skillet, add vinegar and salt and bring to a simmer. Add fish fillets. Cook over low heat for 10 to 15 minutes longer, depending on thickness of fish. Garnish with chopped green onion.

Serve sauce over fish with Mashed Plantains (recipe follows) or boiled rice. Makes 6 servings.

Serve these in place of potatoes for a true Caribbean flavor.

Mashed Plantains

—◆—

2 large semi-ripe plantains (about 1 3/4 pounds unpeeled)
1/4 cup water
1/4 teaspoon salt
1 clove garlic, peeled and crushed through a press
1 cup milk, heated to boiling
1 teaspoon sugar
2 tablespoons butter
1 tablespoon extra virgin olive oil

Peel the plantains by cutting off both ends. Remove one section of the skin lengthwise. Remove remaining skin in strips. Chop the plantains in cubes.

In a medium saucepan, bring the water, salt and garlic to a boil. Add the cubed plantains. Cover and simmer for about 15 to 20 minutes, until the plantains can be pierced easily with a fork, like a boiled potato. Do not allow the water to boil away completely.

In a bowl, mash the plantains, adding the hot milk, sugar, butter and oil.

Makes 6 servings.

How to store fish

• Keep it cold. It's best to make your fish selection when you've finished the rest of your shopping and are ready to pay.

• If you have other errands to run, take an ice chest and a bag of ice for the fish or seafood. Or ask for a separate bag of ice to put on top of the wrapped fish.

• Store in the coldest part of the refrigerator.

• Cook and eat fresh or thawed fish or shellfish within two days of purchase.

• Don't store fillets or steaks in water or in direct contact with ice.

• Place whole fish, fillets or steaks on a cooling rack so the pieces don't overlap. Place the rack over a pan of crushed ice but not in direct contact with it. Cover with plastic wrap or aluminum foil. Drain and re-ice as necessary.

• If you are not able to eat the fish or shellfish within two days, cook it in a microwave oven and freeze it.

When dinner inspiration deserts you, nothing beats a great piece of baked fish in a crusty, herb-flavored coating. Any mild fish is excellent served this way.

Crispy Herb Baked Fish

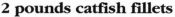

2 pounds catfish fillets
1/2 cup dry unseasoned bread crumbs
3 tablespoons freshly grated
  Parmesan cheese
1/2 teaspoon marjoram or oregano
1/2 teaspoon thyme leaves
1/2 teaspoon freshly ground black
  pepper
4 tablespoons butter or margarine,
  melted

 perch, striped bass, flounder, snapper, orange roughy, kingklip

Preheat oven to 425 F.

Wash the fish fillets, pat them dry with a paper towel and set them aside.

In a pie pan or other shallow dish, combine the bread crumbs, cheese, herbs and pepper. Set aside.

Melt the butter or margarine in a micro-wave-safe baking dish. Dredge the fillets in the melted butter and dip each in the bread crumb mixture. Make sure to coat each fillet. Pat to make sure crumb mixture sticks to fish. Arrange the fillets in a single layer in the dish used to melt the butter (or coat another dish with non-stick cooking spray).

Bake for 12 to 15 minutes until the coating is crispy and golden.

Makes 4 to 6 servings.

Note: For an extra kick, combine the butter with one clove of minced garlic.

Tomatoes, herbs, garlic, olive oil and fresh seafood are a time-honored ingredient mix in the Mediterranean region. This robust dish is not only fast, it's also low in fat and calories.

Mediterranean Microwave Fish

1 1/4 pounds monkfish
1 teaspoon olive oil
1 small red onion, minced (about 1/2 cup)
1 stalk of celery, chopped
2 cloves of garlic, crushed through a press
2 small plum tomatoes or salad tomatoes, seeded and chopped
1 tablespoon chopped parsley
1/2 teaspoon oregano, crushed
1/4 teaspoon salt
1/4 teaspoon freshly ground black pepper
3 tablespoons tomato paste
1/4 cup dry white wine
1/4 cup clam juice
Dash Worcestershire sauce (optional)
Cooked rice, orzo or couscous

 snapper, mahi mahi, cod, tuna, mackerel, orange roughy

Notes: You can prepare this recipe on a conventional range: Heat the olive oil in a non-stick skillet. Saute the onions, celery and garlic for 2 minutes until fragrant. Add the tomatoes, parsley, oregano, tomato paste, wine, clam juice and optional Worcestershire sauce. Bring to a boil and reduce heat to a simmer. Cook for 15 minutes, until the mixture thickens.

Place fish fillets in individual casserole dishes or in one oven-safe baking dish. Top with sauce and bake at 425 degrees for 10 to 12 minutes.

Place the fish fillets in a circle in a microwave-safe baking dish or in individual-serving size oval baking dishes. If the fillets are thin or long, cut into serving portions and fold in half.

In another microwave-safe container, combine the oil, onion, celery, garlic, tomatoes, parsley, oregano, salt and pepper. Cook in the microwave oven on high (100 percent) power for 3 minutes, stirring after 1 1/2 minutes.

Spread the mixture evenly over the fish fillets.

Combine the tomato paste, wine, clam juice and Worcestershire sauce. Pour over the fish and vegetables. Cover loosely with plastic wrap or wax paper. If cooking fish in a single dish, cook on high power (100 percent) for 5 to 6 minutes, turning once.

If cooking fish in individual-serving dishes, cook for 2 to 3 minutes, turning after 1 1/2 minutes. Allow fish to stand in cooking dish at least 3 minutes before serving. Fish will exude liquid during cooking, but most of it will be absorbed as the fish cools.

Serve with cooked rice, orzo or couscous. Orzo, a popular Italian side dish, is rice-shaped pasta. Couscous, a staple of North African cuisine, is granular semolina, similar to pasta. Both are available in ethnic markets and most large grocery stores.

Makes 4 servings.

The tang of orange juice and the nuttiness of pistachios complement the delicate sweetness of the fish.

Stuffed Mahi Mahi with Orange Sauce

1 1/4 pounds mahi mahi fillets
1 tablespoon lemon or orange juice
Non-stick cooking spray, preferably olive oil
3 tablespoons coarsely chopped, shelled pistachio nuts
2 green onions, finely chopped
1 cup soft, fresh bread crumbs
2 tablespoons whole-grain or Dijon-style mustard
2 tablespoons orange juice
1/8 teaspoon black pepper
Orange Sauce (recipe follows)

 flounder, orange roughy, sole, perch, cod, snapper, grouper

Note: Thin fillets can be filled and folded in half and secured with a toothpick. The shape of the fillets will determine whether the fish is rolled around the filling, stuffed inside a pocket or stuffed in a notch.

Select thick mahi mahi fillets and have the fish seller remove the skin. Rinse fish under cold water and pat dry with a paper towel.

Cut the fillets crosswise into 4 even pieces. Slice a horizontal pocket about 1 1/2 inches long through the side of each fillet. (If this is too much trouble, simply slice a V-shaped notch down the center of the fillet.)

Preheat oven to 400 F.

Rub both sides of fish with lemon or orange juice. Lightly coat a baking dish with non-stick cooking spray and arrange fillets in it; refrigerate baking dish while making stuffing.

In a small bowl, combine the pistachio nuts, green onions, bread crumbs, mustard and orange juice. Mix the ingredients until they are moistened and stick together. Form about 2 to 3 tablespoons of the filling into a log and gently stuff the log into the pocket or the notch in the fish.

Bake 15 to 20 minutes, until fish is opaque and stuffing is brown and toasty.

Transfer the fillets to a serving platter and cover with foil to keep warm. Reserve any cooking liquid in the baking dish to add to the sauce.

Serve with rice and a green vegetable, such as sugar snap peas or broccoli.

Makes 4 servings.

Orange Sauce

1 tablespoon unsalted butter
1 tablespoon flour
2 teaspoons freshly grated orange zest
1/2 teaspoon salt
1/4 teaspoon paprika
1 cup evaporated skim milk, heated to almost boiling
1/4 cup fresh orange juice
2 tablespoons white wine
1 tablespoon lemon juice
1 tablespoon Dijon-style mustard

Melt butter in a saucepan. Whisk in flour, salt, paprika and zest. Cook for 1 minute until flour absorbs butter and begins to bubble and brown. Add milk by drops, whisking constantly to avoid lumps. When all the milk has been added, whisk in orange juice, wine and any liquid left in the baking dish after cooking the fish. Cook sauce, stirring constantly, until it thickens.

Remove from heat and whisk in the mustard and lemon juice. Taste for seasonings. If made in advance, the sauce can be warmed over low heat.

Makes about 1 3/4 cups or 8 servings.

Note: To speed things up, heat the evaporated skim milk in a microwave-safe measuring cup for 1 to 2 minutes on high (100 percent power).

To freeze fish:

•Rinse under cold, running water and pat dry with paper towels.
•Wrap tightly in plastic wrap, squeezing out all the air.
•Wrap again in aluminum foil. Write contents and date on a freezer label or strip of masking tape.
•Freeze as quickly as possible.
•For best results, thaw and use within two weeks.

To thaw fish:

•Thaw overnight in the refrigerator.
•Thin fillets and steaks will thaw within 8 to 10 hours in the refrigerator.
•Cook immediately after thawing.

Here is a variation on an Italian dish usually made with veal and ham. This version features a mild fish rolled around a rosy slice of smoked salmon. The cheese sauce tastes rich but is light in calories and fat.

Seafood Saltimbocca in Creamy Cheese Sauce

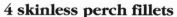

4 skinless perch fillets
4 ounces smoked salmon, thinly sliced
4 sprigs fresh dill or 1/2 teaspoon dried dill, divided
1 tablespoon lemon juice, divided
Non-stick cooking spray
4 teaspoons Parmesan cheese, grated
Parsley for garnish

 sole, orange roughy, flounder

Preheat oven to 400 F. Coat a baking dish with non-stick cooking spray.

Make sure the fillets are thin enough to roll. Place 1 slice of smoked salmon over each fillet of fish. (Save any trimmings or torn pieces of smoked salmon to go in the sauce.) Place a sprig of dill in the middle of each fillet and sprinkle with lemon juice.

Roll fillets like a pinwheel and place seam-side down in the baking dish. Refrigerate while preparing sauce. When ready to serve, bake fillets for 15 to 20 minutes, until fish is opaque and firm to the touch. Reserve cooking liquid to add to Cheese Sauce (recipe follows).

Makes 4 servings.

Cheese Sauce

1 teaspoon canola oil
1 shallot, minced
1 clove garlic, crushed through a press
1/4 teaspoon flour
1/4 teaspoon salt
1/4 teaspoon white pepper
1/4 teaspoon dried dill
1/3 cup clam juice
2 1/2 tablespoons low-calorie,
    whipped cream cheese
3 tablespoons dry white wine
1 teaspoon lemon juice (or to taste)
Hot pepper sauce (optional)

Heat canola oil in a saucepan over medium-low heat. Saute shallot until soft and transparent, about 3 minutes. Add garlic and cook for 1 minute longer. Whisk in flour, salt, white pepper and dill. Cook, stirring constantly until flour begins to adhere to bottom of pan.

Whisk in clam juice, stirring until mixture comes to a boil and thickens. Reduce heat to a simmer. Whisk in cream cheese until it melts. Stir in white wine, lemon juice and fish cooking juices, if any. Adjust seasonings. If desired, add hot pepper sauce and additional lemon juice.

Simmer over low heat for 3 to 5 minutes. Spoon 3 tablespoons of cheese sauce over each fillet. Sprinkle with Parmesan cheese and parsley. If desired, brown under a broiler for 2 minutes.

Makes about 3/4 cup.

Note: You can roll the fish up to 8 hours before cooking and keep it refrigerated. Cooking times will vary depending on thickness of fish.

Remember this recipe on nights when you want something delicious in minutes. Make it with any mild, flaky fish.

Salsa Snapper

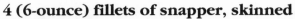

4 (6-ounce) fillets of snapper, skinned
1 teaspoon olive oil
1 medium onion, diced (about 1 cup)
2 garlic cloves, crushed through a
    press
2 medium ripe tomatoes, seeded and
    chopped (about 1 1/4 cups)
1 to 2 pickled jalapeno peppers,
    seeded and minced or 2 tablespoons
    sliced jalapenos, chopped
1 teaspoon dried oregano
1/4 teaspoon cumin
1/4 teaspoon salt
1/4 teaspoon black pepper
2 tablespoons dry white wine
1 tablespoon lime juice
2 tablespoons fresh cilantro, chopped

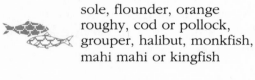 sole, flounder, orange roughy, cod or pollock, grouper, halibut, monkfish, mahi mahi or kingfish

 Substitute commercial Mexican salsa for the homemade sauce in the recipe. Use about 1/4 cup of salsa per fillet and cook according to recipe.

To make salsa mixture, in a microwave-safe baking dish, combine the olive oil, onion, garlic, tomatoes, jalapeno peppers, oregano, cumin, salt and pepper. Stir to mix.

Cover with wax paper and cook on high (100 percent) power for 2 minutes. Stir and cook on high for 2 minutes longer. Nestle the fish fillets in the salsa mixture, spooning some of the mixture over the top. Combine the white wine, lime juice and cilantro and pour over the fillets.

Cover with wax paper and cook on high (100 percent) for 4 minutes. Turn dish and cook 2 minutes longer, until fish is opaque and firm when pressed with the tines of a fork.

Allow to stand 3 minutes before serving so the fish can absorb the liquid it gives off during cooking.

Serve fillets next to Mexican-Style Pilaf (recipe follows). Spoon salsa mixture over both.

Makes 4 servings.

Note: The dish can also be cooked in a conventional oven. Preheat oven to 350 F. In a non-stick skillet, heat the olive oil and saute the onions, garlic, tomatoes, jalapeno peppers, cumin and oregano for 5 minutes or until tender. Add the white wine, lime juice, cilantro, salt and pepper. Simmer. Arrange the fillets in a baking dish and pour the salsa mixture on top. Cover and bake for 20 to 25 minutes, until the fish is opaque and firm when pressed with the tines of a fork. Serve with rice. This dish is also excellent served cold.

Mexican-Style Pilaf

1 cup rice
1/4 teaspoon salt
1/4 teaspoon black pepper
3 dashes hot sauce (or to taste)
1 (16-ounce) can whole peeled
   tomatoes, with juice
3/4 cup water

In a large saucepan, combine rice, salt, black pepper and hot sauce. Crush the tomatoes with a spoon and chop them into large pieces. Stir the crushed tomatoes, their juice and water into the rice mixture. Bring to a simmer. Simmer for 10 to 12 minutes on medium-low heat. Stir occasionally to make sure mixture isn't scorching. Turn off heat and allow rice to stand, covered, for 5 minutes.

Serve hot with fish.

Makes 4 servings.

What's fish oil?

For most health-conscious Americans, fat tops the list of dirty nutritional words. But there's bad fat and there's good fat. Fish fat, found in the natural oils in the meat, is a good, healthful variety that helps clean fatty substances out of the blood.

Fish oil contains substances called omega-3 fatty acids. Researchers believe omega-3 fatty acids help lower levels of cholesterol and triglycerides, two types of fat that circulate in the blood. Fish oil is also credited with reducing high blood pressure, "thinning" the blood to reduce chances of clots and boosting the body's natural immune system.

You can get the benefits of fish oil by eating fish or seafood two or three times a week.

All fish contain some fish oil but certain species contain more than others. Oily fish are usually cold-water varieties that have dark or pink meat. Mackerel, salmon, tuna and trout contain more omega-3 fatty acids than snowy white cod, flounder, perch or red snapper. And in general, saltwater fish contain more natural fish oils than freshwater fish. Oil content also will vary according to the time of year and the fish's diet.

The amount of natural fish oil affects the flavor of the meat as well. Fish with higher levels of oil in their flesh have more robust flavor. Salmon, herring, sablefish, pompano and mackerel all have rich, distinctive flavors and contain more natural oil.

Gruyere is the ultimate Swiss cheese for cheese lovers. Its rich, nutty flavor really adds dimension to this quiche. This is a great item to take to a potluck.

Seafood Quiche

1 commercially prepared pie crust, large enough to fit a 9-inch pie plate
1 cup shredded Gruyere or Swiss cheese
1/4 teaspoon dill
1/4 teaspoon tarragon
6 ounces flaked imitation crab
3 eggs
1/2 teaspoon salt
1/4 teaspoon white pepper
1/8 teaspoon paprika
1 cup half-and-half
1 cup milk

 shrimp, scallops, real crab meat or lobster

Preheat oven to 375 F.

Press pie crust in a 9-inch pie plate. Crimp the edges to form a decorative border.

Toss the imitation crab with the cheese, dill and tarragon. Spread the mixture evenly over the bottom of the pie shell. In a mixing bowl, beat the eggs with the half-and-half, milk, salt, pepper and paprika. Make sure the salt dissolves in the liquid.

Pour the egg mixture over the seafood. Place in the lowest rack of the oven and bake for 15 minutes.

Reduce oven temperature to 325 F. Bake for 30 minutes longer, until center of the quiche is set or until a knife blade inserted in the center comes out clean.

Allow quiche to stand at room temperature for 10 to 15 minutes before slicing. It can also be served chilled or at room temperature.

Makes 8 servings.

Note: If you substitute other fish or seafood in this recipe, cook it first or have it steamed at the fish market. Raw seafood will give off moisture and make the quiche watery and the crust soggy.

Tahini, a Middle Eastern sesame seed paste, gives this dish a rich, smooth flavor. Apricots in the stuffing provide a touch of tartness.

Baked Fish With Apricot Couscous

1 pound flaky fish fillets
2 tablespoons low-sodium soy sauce
   or tamari
1 tablespoon fresh ginger, grated
2 tablespoons tahini (sesame seed
   paste)
1 tablespoon lemon juice
2 cups plus 1 tablespoon boiling water
1 cup couscous
7 dried apricots, diced (about 1/4 cup)
1/4 teaspoon salt
1 medium onion, finely chopped
   (about 1 cup)
1/4 cup parsley, minced
Non-stick cooking spray
1 teaspoon Oriental sesame oil

flounder, orange roughy,
catfish, cod, hake, kingfish

Preheat oven to 350 F.

Mix soy sauce, ginger, tahini, lemon juice and 1 tablespoon of the boiling water to make a creamy paste.

Pour mixture over fish, making sure each fillet is evenly coated. Marinate fish in refrigerator for 20 minutes to one hour.

Meanwhile, prepare the couscous stuffing. In a medium bowl combine the couscous, diced apricots and salt. Pour the remaining 2 cups boiling water over the mixture and allow to stand until all the water is absorbed, about 15 minutes. Stir in the minced onion and parsley.

Stir in any marinade that doesn't cling to the fish.

Coat a large baking dish or 5 individual oval baking dishes with non-stick cooking spray. Mound the couscous in the prepared baking dishes and lay the fish fillets on top. Drizzle each fillet lightly with sesame oil.

Bake for 20 to 30 minutes, depending on thickness of fillets. Serve hot with a green vegetable such as zucchini, Brussels sprouts, broccoli or spinach.

Makes 5 servings.

Note: Tahini is available in Middle Eastern markets and health food stores. The best-tasting brands are made with 100 percent sesame oil and crushed sesame seeds. Inferior brands are made with crushed sesame seeds mixed with vegetable oil.

Couscous, a type of pasta popular in Morocco, is also available in health food stores, Middle Eastern markets and some grocery stores. A whole-wheat variety is also available.

Farm-raised catfish is always fresh and delicious. It has a mild flavor because it lives in clean water and is fed a controlled diet. This is a mild curry with slightly sweet overtones from the apple. If a spicier curry is desired, add more curry and chili powders.

Curried Catfish with Shrimp

4 catfish fillets (about 4 to 6 ounces each)

1/2 teaspoon salt

1 tablespoon peanut oil or canola oil

1 teaspoon fresh ginger, finely minced

1 clove garlic, crushed through a press

1/4 teaspoon cumin powder

1/4 teaspoon coriander

Pinch (or to taste) hot red pepper powder, such as cayenne

2 heaping tablespoons good-quality curry powder

2 teaspoons flour

1 small golden delicious apple, cored and grated (about 1 cup)

1 teaspoon sugar

1 tablespoon apple cider or rice vinegar

8 medium shrimp, shelled and deveined

Cooked brown rice

 flounder, sole, perch, turbot, pollock, haddock

Note: The fish and the sauce can be made in advance and assembled before serving. Refrigerate until ready to serve. Reheat in the microwave oven on high (100 percent) power for 2 minutes. Cook under the oven broiler for 2 minutes longer.

In a glass baking dish, arrange the fillets with the thickest part to the outside. Sprinkle evenly with salt. Cover loosely with plastic wrap. Cook on high (100 percent) power for 4 minutes. Turn dish and cook for 4 minutes longer. Fish should be opaque.

Allow fish to stand for 4 minutes.

Pour off and measure the accumulated cooking juices from the fish. Liquid should equal about 1/2 to 2/3 cup. If there is less, add water or apple juice to equal 2/3 cup. Set liquid aside while preparing sauce.

In a saucepan over medium heat, cook the ginger in the oil for 1 minute. Add the garlic and cook for 1 minute longer. In a small bowl, combine the cumin, coriander, hot pepper powder, curry powder and flour. Sprinkle over the ginger mixture. Whisk constantly until spices are dark and fragrant and ingredients are thoroughly mixed. Pour the reserved cooking liquid into the mixture, whisking constantly until the mixture thickens. Stir in the apple, vinegar and sugar. Simmer over low heat for 4 to 5 minutes to allow flavors to blend. Remove from heat.

Preheat the oven broiler. Pour the sauce over the cooked fillets. If any extra cooking liquid from the fish has accumulated during the standing period, stir it into the sauce. Garnish fish with shrimp.

Broil about 4 inches from the heat source for 2 to 3 minutes, until shrimp are pink and tightly curled and sauce develops a glazed patina. Serve hot with brown rice and a green vegetable.

Makes 4 servings.

Catfish is the sole of the South. Lemon and cornmeal show it off.

Crunchy Citrus Catfish

Non-stick cooking spray
4 catfish fillets (about 1 1/2 pounds)
2 tablespoons olive oil
4 tablespoons yellow cornmeal
2 tablespoons flour
1 teaspoon freshly grated lemon rind
(1 small lemon, yellow part of the
rind only)
1 teaspoon dried thyme leaves
1/4 teaspoon sage
1/4 teaspoon salt
1/4 teaspoon white pepper

 orange roughy, perch, turbot, trout

Preheat oven to 400 F.

Coat a baking dish with non-stick cooking spray. Brush both sides of the fillets with olive oil.

In a shallow plate, combine the cornmeal, flour, lemon rind, thyme, sage, salt and pepper. Mix well.

Dredge the oiled fish in the cornmeal mixture, coating well. Arrange the fillets without touching in the prepared baking dish.

Bake for 12 minutes or until the fish is firm to the touch when pressed on the top. If fish doesn't brown sufficiently, heat the oven broiler and cook about 4 inches from the flame for 2 to 4 minutes.

Allow to stand for a few minutes before removing from pan.

Serve with Old Fashioned Tartar Sauce (recipe page 200), Mango Salsa (recipe page 198) or Cocktail Sauce (recipe page 196).

Makes 4 servings.

I first made this dish with chicken and then discovered how much better it is with fish. The sesame seeds look like golden sequins after they're cooked. You can coat the fillets in advance and refrigerate them on wax paper until you're ready to cook.

Sequined Snapper

1 1/4 pounds snapper fillets
1/3 cup flour
1/2 teaspoon salt
1 egg
2 tablespoons low-fat milk
6 tablespoons sesame seeds
1 tablespoon canola oil
3 tablespoons balsamic vinegar
6 tablespoons white wine
1/2 teaspoon Oriental sesame oil

 mahi mahi, shark, trout, orange roughy, sea bass

Rinse the fish and pat dry. Sprinkle with the salt. Dredge the fillets in the flour.

In a shallow bowl that is large enough to accommodate the fillets, beat the egg and milk together. Place the sesame seeds in another bowl or on a plate. Dip the fish in the egg mixture and again in the sesame seeds.

Heat the canola oil in a large non-stick skillet. Add the fillets and cook over medium-high heat for 5 minutes on each side, until the sesame seeds are golden brown. Do not cook over too hot a burner or the seeds may scorch.

Remove the fish to a heated platter or individual plates.

Place the skillet used for cooking the fish back on the heat. Add the balsamic vinegar, white wine and sesame oil. Bring to a boil, stirring constantly. Boil for 2 to 3 minutes until liquid has reduced slightly. Pour sauce over fish.

Makes 4 servings.

I'm crazy about the combination of fish and nuts. Use your favorite kind in this easy dish – I like Brazil nuts.

Baked Catfish Fillets

4 catfish fillets
2 tablespoons milk
3 tablespoons Dijon mustard
1/4 teaspoon cayenne pepper
1 cup ground Brazil nuts, walnuts, pecans or peanuts

Preheat oven to 400 F.

In a shallow bowl, combine milk, Dijon mustard and cayenne pepper. Dip fillets into this mixture. Then dip into ground nuts, shaking off excess. Coat a baking sheet lightly with non-stick cooking spray. Bake for 10 to 12 minutes or until fish flakes and nuts are brown.

Makes 4 servings.

Cooked is better

For healthy adults, nothing may be wrong with gulping an occasional raw oyster on the half-shell straight from the sea. But in general, I believe people should avoid eating raw fish and shellfish just as they avoid raw chicken or pork. Pregnant women and people who are weak due to illness, surgery or diseases of the immune system, should avoid eating uncooked and undercooked fish and shellfish.

Like chicken or pork, uncooked fish and shellfish can harbor potentially harmful bacteria, parasites and viruses. The heat of cooking kills these organisms and makes the food wholesome and healthful.

Water pollution and environmental pollution caused by natural toxicants also can cause contamination in fish. While cases of illness caused by contamination are rare, they happen if fish and seafood are harvested from polluted waters.

To prevent contaminated fish from reaching consumers, the Food and Drug Administration inspects fish processing plants and docks where imported seafood is unloaded. State organizations monitor water purity to ensure that shellfish are not harvested from polluted waters. In 1991, the FDA expanded its inspection program and opened an Office of Seafood to maintain seafood safety standards.

The best protection for consumers against food-borne illness from fish and seafood is cooking. So fire up the frying pan, the microwave oven or the grill and leave raw fish and seafood alone.

When you're really pressed for time, buy the vegetables pre-cut from the salad bar in the supermarket. You can jazz up the sauce as much as you like with the optional ginger, garlic and hot pepper.

Baked Potatoes with Sweet and Sour Crab and Vegetables

2 medium baking potatoes (about 8 ounces each)
8 ounces imitation crab meat
1 tablespoon peanut or canola oil
1 teaspoon minced fresh ginger (optional)
1/2 cup onion, sliced into strips
1 carrot, peeled and sliced into thin strips
1 stalk celery, sliced into strips
1 cup broccoli florets
1/4 cup water
1/2 cup red, yellow or green bell pepper, sliced into strips
1/4 cup canned bamboo shoots
1 clove garlic, crushed through a press (optional)
1/4 cup cider vinegar
3 tablespoons brown sugar
2 tablespoons soy sauce
1 teaspoon sesame oil
2 teaspoons cornstarch mixed with 1 tablespoon water
1/8 teaspoon crushed hot pepper or a few drops hot pepper sauce (optional)

 crab meat, shrimp, scallops

Notes: If desired, substitute snow peas for the bell pepper or baby corn for the bamboo shoots. Substitute frozen vegetables for this recipe if desired. However, reduce the cooking times to prevent the vegetables from overcooking.

Scrub the potatoes thoroughly. Pierce with a knife or a fork and arrange in a microwave-safe baking dish. Cover and bake on high (100 percent power) 18 minutes, turning once. Potatoes are done when they give to gentle pressure. Allow to stand for 5 to 10 minutes, covered with a towel. Assemble the imitation crab meat, onion, carrot, celery, broccoli, peppers and bamboo shoots near the stove. If using ginger, place it near the stove also. In a measuring cup, combine the vinegar, brown sugar, soy sauce, sesame oil and optional pepper and garlic. Stir well to dissolve sugar.

In a small bowl, stir together cornstarch and water. Set aside.

In a large skillet or wok, heat the oil until very hot. Add the onion, carrot and broccoli and stir-fry about 5 minutes, or until the vegetables are crisp-tender. Add the water and cook 3 minutes longer. Add the imitation crab meat, bell pepper strips, bamboo shoots and sweet-and-sour sauce. Cook for 3 minutes, until the mixture comes to a boil. Add the cornstarch. When sauce mixture begins to thicken, immediately remove from heat.

Split the potatoes in half and place cut side up on two dinner plates. Divide the sauce, imitation crab meat and vegetable mixture in half and pour on top. Serve warm.

Makes 2 servings.

Alligator has a fine sweet, meaty flavor. It can be tough but it's terrific when ground, as it is in these light, flavorful seafood burgers. It is often available frozen in fish markets.

Gator Burgers or Nuggets

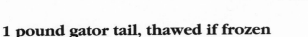

1 pound gator tail, thawed if frozen
   and drained
1/2 cup celery, diced
4 green onions, finely diced (about
   1/2 cup)
2 cups whole-wheat bread crumbs
   (4 slices bread)
2 egg whites
2 tablespoons mayonnaise
1 tablespoon good-quality mustard
1/4 teaspoon cayenne pepper
1 tablespoon ketchup
1 teaspoon fresh lime juice
1/2 teaspoon salt
1/2 teaspoon freshly ground black
   pepper
1/4 cup all-purpose flour
Peanut or canola oil for frying

conch

In a meat grinder or food processor, grind the gator tail until it is the consistency of chopped clams. Pick through it to remove any bits of tough sinew. Combine with celery, green onions, crumbs, egg whites, mayonnaise, mustard, cayenne, ketchup, lime juice and salt, pepper and flour. Mix until ingredients stick together. Shape into medium-sized, thin patties. Place on a baking sheet and refrigerate for 30 minutes.

Fry in a skillet in a small amount of oil until golden. Burgers also can be grilled. Turn with a large pancake turner to prevent breaking.

If desired, serve on whole-wheat kaiser rolls with lettuce and tomato.

Makes 6 servings.

Notes: To make baked Gator Nuggets for appetizers, use a teaspoon to drop small balls of burger mixture on lightly oiled baking sheets. Preheat oven to 350 F. Bake for 14 to 16 minutes, until the balls are golden brown and firm to the touch. Serve hot or allow to cool to room temperature and freeze until ready to serve. The nuggets taste spicier with cayenne than do the burgers.

Serve with Cocktail Sauce (recipe page 196), Old Fashioned Tartar Sauce (recipe page 200), Fiesty Apricot Sauce (recipe page 21) or Pepper Jelly Sauce (recipe page 8).

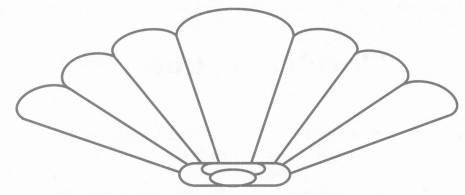

PASTA, PIZZA AND SANDWICHES

A creamy, dreamy seafood dish with a delicate undercurrent of orange zest. The citrus cuts the richness.

Floridian Fettuccine

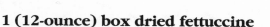

1 (12-ounce) box dried fettuccine
3/4 pound large shrimp, shelled and deveined
1/2 pound bay scallops
1 tablespoon butter
2 shallots, finely chopped
1 tablespoon flour
1/2 teaspoon salt
1/4 teaspoon white pepper
2 teaspoons freshly grated orange rind (about 1 medium orange)
1 cup milk
3 tablespoons orange juice or white wine
1 tablespoon orange liqueur
1/4 cup heavy cream
1 tablespoon lemon juice
2 tablespoons minced fresh chives or green onions

 cubed tuna, shark or swordfish, crab meat

Heat a large kettle of salted water until boiling. Add the pasta and cook according to package directions until tender but not mushy. Drain and reserve.

While pasta is cooking, melt the butter in a large non-stick skillet. Stir in the shallots and saute for 1 to 2 minutes. Sprinkle the flour, salt, pepper and orange rind over the shallots and stir to coat evenly. Cook, stirring for 1 minute. Stir in the milk and cook, stirring until the mixture comes to a boil and thickens.

Add the shrimp, orange juice or white wine and cream. Simmer the mixture together for 2 to 3 minutes, until the shrimp turn pink and begin to curl. Stir the scallops, orange liqueur and lemon juice into the mixture. Cook briefly and taste for seasonings. Add more salt, wine or lemon juice to sharpen flavor if necessary.

Divide cooked pasta among four plates. Spoon sauce and seafood over pasta and sprinkle with chives or green onions.

Makes 4 servings.

This creamy recipe only tastes fattening. It's low in fat and calories and can be made in minutes, especially if you use fresh pasta.

Fettuccine with Salmon and Mushrooms

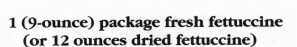

1 (9-ounce) package fresh fettuccine (or 12 ounces dried fettuccine)
1 teaspoon olive oil
2 green onions, minced
4 ounces fresh mushrooms, wiped clean and sliced
1 large clove garlic, crushed through a press
1 teaspoon flour
1 (13-ounce) can evaporated skim milk
1 1/2 ounces reduced-calorie cream cheese (1/2 of a 3-ounce package)
1/4 teaspoon salt
1/8 teaspoon white pepper
1 (7 1/2-ounce) can red salmon, bones and skin discarded, juice reserved
2 tablespoons fresh parsley, minced (optional)
Lemon wedges (optional)

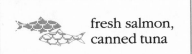
fresh salmon, canned tuna

Place a large kettle of salted water over high heat to boil. Cook the fettuccine according to package directions. Fresh pasta cooks in about 2 minutes; dried pasta cooks in about 9 minutes. Drain and set aside.

In a non-stick skillet, heat the olive oil and add the green onions and mushrooms. Cook over medium heat for 5 minutes, until onions are tender and lightly browned. Add the garlic and flour and stir to coat vegetables for 1 minute.

Add the evaporated skim milk a little at a time, stirring until the sauce begins to simmer and thicken. Add the juice from the canned salmon and the cream cheese. Stir until the cheese melts.

Stir in the salmon and parsley. Heat 2 minutes longer. Divide pasta into four portions and top with equal amounts of sauce. Serve warm.

Makes 4 servings.

Pasta and tomato sauce are delicious complements for crab. The light, thin sauce turns a lovely pink hue when cooked. Imitation crab, or surimi, also tastes great in this recipe.

Pasta with Crab Meat and Tomatoes

1 (12-ounce) container lump crab meat, picked over carefully to remove shells and cartilage
1 tablespoon olive oil
2 green onions, chopped
1 clove garlic, crushed through a press
3 ripe tomatoes, seeded and chopped
2 tablespoons tomato paste
1/2 cup white wine
1 cup chicken broth or clam juice
1/4 cup heavy cream
1 tablespoon finely chopped fresh parsley
1 tablespoon finely chopped fresh basil
1/4 teaspoon white pepper
12 ounces hot pasta, cooked and drained
Fresh basil or parsley, chopped, for garnish

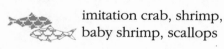 imitation crab, shrimp, baby shrimp, scallops

Pick through the crab and set aside.

Heat the oil in a non-stick skillet. Add the green onions and garlic. Saute until the onion is translucent, about 3 to 4 minutes.

Add tomatoes and tomato paste and cook for 5 minutes. Stir in the white wine, chicken stock or clam juice, cream, parsley, basil, pepper and crab. Bring mixture to a simmer. Cook on medium low heat for 10 minutes.

Spoon the hot sauce over the cooked pasta.

Makes 4 to 6 servings.

Notes: If you want a thicker sauce, add 2 teaspoons of cornstarch mixed with 1 tablespoon of water to the sauce during the last minute of the 10-minute simmering. Stir in the cornstarch and remove the sauce from heat when it begins to boil. Serve over hot pasta as directed.

This country-style Thai dish is popular in restaurants. The combination of peanuts and seafood is exquisite. "Pad" means noodles in the Thai language.

Pad Thai

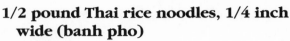

1/2 pound Thai rice noodles, 1/4 inch wide (banh pho)
Hot water
3/4 pound medium shrimp, shelled and deveined and cut in half
1 tablespoon nam pla (Thai fish sauce)
3 tablespoons sugar
3 tablespoons water
1/4 cup white-wine or cider vinegar
1 tablespoon tomato paste
1 tablespoon hoisin sauce
1 tablespoon chunky peanut butter
2 cloves garlic, crushed through a press
1/8 teaspoon ground, dried red chilies (optional)
2 tablespoons peanut oil
4 green onions, sliced in 1/2-inch lengths
2 cups bean sprouts
1/4 cup roasted unsalted peanuts, chopped
1 lime cut into wedges

Soak noodles for 30 minutes in hot water to cover. They should be flexible but not mushy. Use kitchen shears to cut the noodles into 4-inch lengths; drain well.

Make sauce by combining nam pla, sugar, water, vinegar, tomato paste, hoisin, peanut butter and garlic. Mix well. Heat the sauce for 1 minute in a microwave oven to simplify mixing the peanut butter. Heat oil in a wok or a heavy skillet. Add green onions and shrimp and stir-fry briefly, until shrimp turn pink and curl up. Add drained noodles and toss to coat with cooking oil.

Pour in the sauce and bring to a boil. Gently fold in the noodles until they absorb the sauce, about 3 to 4 minutes. Push the noodle mixture to one side. Add the bean sprouts and stir into the noodles. Cook about 1 minute. Remove to a platter. Sprinkle with the chopped peanuts.

Serve with lime squeezed over each portion.

Makes 4 servings.

Notes: The rice noodles, fish sauce and bean sprouts are available in Oriental markets. Wide noodles are traditional, but thin rice vermicelli can be substituted.

If scallops aren't in the market, make this meal-in-one-dish with shrimp, mussels or freshly shucked oysters.

Pasta with Scallops and Vegetables

3/4 pound bay or sea scallops
9 ounces fresh white or spinach
    fettuccine or 12 ounces dried
    fettuccine
2 cups broccoli florets
1 tablespoon olive oil
2 cloves garlic, crushed through a
    press
1/2 cup diced yellow or red bell
    pepper
4 ounces mushrooms, sliced (about
    1 1/2 cups)
1/4 cup dry white wine
1/2 cup chicken broth or commercial
    clam juice
1/4 teaspoon white pepper
1/4 teaspoon nutmeg
1/4 teaspoon salt
1 teaspoon cornstarch
2 teaspoons lemon juice

Tip: Scallops are often sandy. To get rid of the sand, fill a bowl with cold water and dump in the scallops. Swish the scallops in the water and pick them up in your hands, allowing the water to drain between your fingers. Sand is heavier than water and will fall to the bottom of the bowl. If a lot of sand has accumulated in the bowl, it may be a good idea to rinse the scallops a second and third time.

Bring 2 quarts of salted water to a boil. Add the fettuccine or other pasta and return to a boil. If using fresh pasta, add the broccoli florets when the water returns to boiling. Cook 3 to 5 minutes, or according to package directions.

If using dried pasta, cook the pasta for 5 minutes, then add the broccoli florets and cook for 4 to 5 minutes longer. Drain.

Heat the olive oil in a large, non-stick skillet over medium heat. Add the garlic and saute 1 minute, until fragrant. Add the diced peppers and mushrooms. Cook, stirring constantly for 3 to 4 minutes, or until mushrooms darken and the peppers begin to soften. Stir in the scallops and any juice that has accumulated around them. Cook for 2 minutes, until scallops begin to turn opaque. Stir in the white wine and broth. Add the white pepper, nutmeg and salt.

Bring liquid to a simmer and cook for 3 to 4 minutes longer. In a small container, combine the cornstarch and lemon juice to make a smooth paste. Stir this into the scallop mixture and cook for 30 seconds or until the sauce thickens slightly.

Transfer the warm pasta and broccoli to a large serving bowl. Pour the scallop mixture over pasta and toss to coat every strand.

Serve warm with toasted bread. If desired, sprinkle with Parmesan cheese.

Makes 4 servings.

A recipe kids are sure to love because it is mild and creamy.

Baked Ziti and Crab Casserole

1 (16-ounce) box ziti
16 ounces pasteurized crab meat
1 (10 1/2-ounce) can Cheddar cheese
   soup
1 1/2 cups low-fat milk
1 teaspoon dill
1 teaspoon marjoram
1 teaspoon onion powder
4 dashes hot sauce
1 1/2 cups shredded sharp white
   Cheddar or Muenster cheese
4 tablespoons grated Parmesan cheese

 imitation crab, baby or small shrimp, oysters, clam strips, mussels

 Make the casserole in advance and refrigerate up to 3 days before baking. You can also make these in individual portions. They will bake in about 15 minutes.

Preheat oven to 350 F. Coat a 2-quart casserole or 2 1-quart casseroles with non-stick cooking spray. Set aside.

Bring a kettle of salted water to a boil and cook the pasta according to package directions. Do not overcook. Drain the pasta and set aside.

While pasta is cooking, pick through the crab to remove any bits of shell or cartilage. Stir the crab into the pasta. Mix the cheese soup and milk together. Add the dill, marjoram, onion powder, hot sauce and shredded cheese. Pour into prepared dish. Sprinkle top with Parmesan cheese. Bake for 30 minutes until bubbling and brown on top.

Makes 12 servings.

Fast, colorful and delicious. The creamy sauce really enhances the thin pasta.

Pasta with Catfish and Artichokes

2 catfish fillets
3 tablespoons butter
1 (10-ounce) package frozen artichoke
hearts, thawed, drained and sliced
1 red pepper, cut in julienne strips
1 carrot, cut in julienne strips
1 zucchini, cut in julienne strips
2/3 cup heavy cream
1/2 cup grated Parmesan cheese,
divided
1/4 teaspoon ground nutmeg
8 ounces angel hair pasta, vermicelli
or extra thin spaghetti

scallops, squid rings, cubes of tuna or swordfish

Cut catfish in half crosswise and slice into thin strips. Saute catfish in melted butter; add artichokes, red pepper, carrot strips and zucchini. Cook until tender. Stir in heavy cream, half the Parmesan cheese and nutmeg. Bring to a boil and remove from heat. Keep warm.

Cook pasta according to package directions, drain. Toss with cream and fish mixture. Sprinkle remaining cheese on top.

Makes 4 servings.

Without the traditional layer of tomato sauce, so-called white pizzas really show off the flavor of the toppings. Yellow tomatoes, also called low-acid tomatoes, are sweeter and firmer than red tomatoes. I love the sunshine-yellow color and delicate flavor. If you can't find yellow tomatoes, use red tomatoes and yellow peppers.

Shrimp, Red Pepper and Yellow Tomato Pizza

12 large shrimp, shelled and deveined
1 prepared pizza crust
2 tablespoons garlic oil (see Tip) or olive oil
2 cups grated part-skim mozzarella cheese
1 teaspoon dried marjoram or oregano
1/4 teaspoon dried dill
1 yellow tomato, cored and thinly sliced
1 red pepper, seeded and cut into thin rings
1/2 cup Jarlsberg or other Swiss cheese

Tip: Garlic oil is easy to make and handy to have in the refrigerator when you want garlic flavor but don't need a whole clove. Pour 1/3 cup olive oil in a jar with a tight-fitting lid. Press 1 large clove garlic into the oil. Refrigerate and allow the oil to steep for up to three weeks. Replace oil after one month or it will become too strong. Use only for cooking and keep refrigerated at all times.

Preheat oven to 425 F.

Place the shrimp in a microwave-safe baking dish. Cook on medium (50 percent) power for 1 to 2 minutes, until shrimp curl slightly. Remove from oven and drain. Do not overcook, because shrimp will cook longer in oven.

Brush pizza crust with garlic oil or olive oil. Spread the mozzarella cheese evenly over the crust. Sprinkle evenly with marjoram and dill. Cover the cheese with slices of the tomato and arrange shrimp evenly over the tomato. Top with rings of red pepper. Sprinkle with Jarlsberg or Swiss cheese.

Bake for 8 minutes or according to package directions. Allow to stand at least 5 minutes before cutting.

Makes 4 servings.

Notes: Use one of the several brands of commercially prepared pizza crusts on the market these days.

My husband developed this pizza and dubbed it "The Tornado" because it's a whirl of sharp, salty flavors.

Salmon, Caper and Blue Cheese Pizza

1 prepared pizza crust

1 tablespoon garlic oil or olive oil (page 173)

2 cups grated part-skim mozzarella cheese

1 (7 1/2 ounce) can red salmon, drained, skin and bones removed

1/2 teaspoon dill

2 small roma or plum tomatoes, seeded and finely chopped

1 teaspoon capers, drained

2 ounces Danish or other blue cheese, crumbled

 canned tuna, canned shrimp, sardines, smoked oysters

Preheat oven to 425 F.

Brush prepared pizza crust with garlic oil or olive oil. Spread the mozzarella evenly over the crust. Flake the salmon over the cheese and sprinkle surface evenly with dill, chopped tomatoes and capers. Top evenly with blue cheese.

Bake 8 minutes or according to package directions. Allow to stand at least 5 minutes before cutting.

Makes 4 servings.

Notes: Use one of the several brands of commercially prepared pizza crusts on the market these days. Roma or plum tomatoes are oblong or oval rather than round like salad tomatoes. They have fewer seeds than salad tomatoes.

White Cheddar is less oily than regular Cheddar cheese so it cooks better on pizza. If the flavor is too sharp for your taste, substitute Havarti or Muenster cheese for the Cheddar.

Shrimp, Herb and Baby Corn Pizza

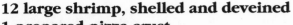

12 large shrimp, shelled and deveined

1 prepared pizza crust

1 tablespoon garlic oil (page 173) or olive oil

2 cups grated part-skim mozzarella cheese

1/4 cup finely chopped fresh parsley

1/4 cup finely chopped fresh basil

1/4 teaspoon freshly ground black pepper

8 spears of baby corn, packed in brine

1/2 cup grated sharp white Cheddar cheese

 canned tuna, canned salmon, cooked scallops, imitation crab meat, smoked baby clams

Arrange the shrimp in a microwave-safe baking dish. Cook on medium (50 percent) power for 1 to 2 minutes, until shrimp begin to curl. Drain and set aside. Do not overcook because shrimp will continue to cook in the oven.

Brush prepared pizza crust with garlic oil or olive oil. Spread mozzarella cheese evenly over crust. Sprinkle parsley, basil and pepper evenly over cheese. Arrange baby corn in spokes around the crust and place a few shrimp between each ear of corn. Spread grated sharp white Cheddar over surface of pizza.

Bake 8 minutes or according to package directions. Allow to stand at least 5 minutes before cutting.

Makes 4 servings.

Notes: Use one of the several brands of commercially prepared pizza crusts on the market these days. If you don't have fresh herbs, substitute 1/2 teaspoon each of dried herbs.

For a true Florida flavor, cook the fish in your trusty cast-iron skillet.

Grouper Sandwich
with Curried Mayonnaise

1 1/4 pounds grouper fillets, about
  1 inch thick
1/4 teaspoon salt
1/4 teaspoon pepper
1/4 teaspoon ground cumin
2 tablespoons oil
1 tablespoon butter
Onion hamburger buns or sub rolls
Lettuce, tomato and sliced purple
  onion, for garnish
Curried Mayonnaise (recipe page 199)

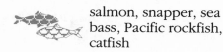 salmon, snapper, sea bass, Pacific rockfish, catfish

Cut fish into even portions, slightly larger than the hamburger buns or sub rolls. Combine the salt, pepper and cumin in a small dish. Sprinkle evenly over both sides of the fillets.

Heat the oil and butter in a large skillet. When butter begins to foam, add the fillets and saute for 5 minutes on one side. Turn with a large spatula and saute 4 minutes on the other side. Fish is done when it is firm to the touch.

While fish is cooking, spread buns or rolls with Curried Mayonnaise. Toast under the oven broiler until bread is crusty and golden.

Garnish sandwiches with lettuce, tomato and onion. Serve extra Curried Mayonnaise on the side.

Makes 4 servings.

Palmer Yergey, who owned a restaurant in Winter Park, Florida, gave me the idea for these terrific fish sandwiches. He made them with gator. The slaw tastes like crunchy tartar sauce but you can also top the sandwiches with Cocktail Sauce or Mango Salsa.

Fish "Dogs" with Slaw Topping

1 pound mahi mahi
1/4 cup milk
1/2 cup cornmeal
1/2 teaspoon salt
1/2 teaspoon lemon pepper
1/2 teaspoon chili powder or Cajun
   spice blend
4 tablespoons canola or peanut oil
6 hot dog buns or sourdough hoagie
   rolls, buttered lightly and toasted
Cole Slaw Topping (recipe follows)

 tuna, grouper, halibut, haddock, butterfish, catfish

Cut the fish into strips about the size of a hot dog. Pour the milk in a shallow dish. Combine the cornmeal, salt, lemon pepper and chili powder in another shallow dish. Dip each piece of fish in milk and roll in cornmeal-spice mixture.

Heat the oil in a heavy skillet. When hot, fry the fish dogs without crowding, turning occasionally. Fish will take about 6 to 8 minutes to cook, depending on thickness of fish. Don't overcook. Set aside on paper towels to drain.

Serve hot in toasted buns with about 1/4 cup of Cole Slaw Topping spooned on top.

Makes 6 servings.

This is an excellent salad with or without the Fish Dogs!

Cole Slaw Topping

**12 ounces shredded cole slaw mix or
2 1/2 cups shredded green and red
cabbage**

2 green onions, finely chopped

**1/4 cup frozen green peas, thawed
and drained**

1 cup mayonnaise

3 tablespoons cider vinegar

3 teaspoons sugar

1 teaspoon Worcestershire sauce

**1 teaspoon dried dill or 2 tablespoons
fresh chopped dill**

1/4 teaspoon salt

Combine the slaw mix or shredded cabbage, green onions and green peas in a large bowl. In a separate container, combine the mayonnaise, vinegar, sugar, Worcestershire sauce, salt and dill. Stir until sugar and salt dissolve. Pour over slaw mixture and toss to combine. Refrigerate until ready to serve.

Makes 8 servings.

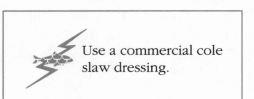 Use a commercial cole slaw dressing.

This is an easy and outstanding variation on the famous New Orleans sandwich creation called a muffuletta. This sandwich has fresh tuna, sliced tomato and a robust olive relish on round slices of bread. Wedges of the sandwich are toasted in olive oil and served like slices of double-crust pizza.

My Tuna Muffuletta

1 pound tuna, sliced into 1/4-inch steaks
4 tablespoons olive oil, divided
1 clove garlic
1/3 cup green olives with pimento stuffing (about 8 jumbo)
1/3 cup pitted black olives (about 14 small)
1 tablespoon chopped parsley
3 tablespoons mayonnaise
1 tablespoon mustard
1 round loaf peasant-style bread, sliced horizontally into 1/4-inch circles
1 large ripe tomato, sliced

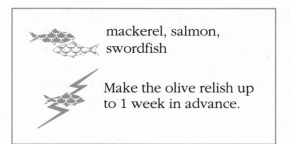

mackerel, salmon, swordfish

Make the olive relish up to 1 week in advance.

To make the relish: In a blender or food processor, chop the garlic and parsley into fine mince. Add 1 tablespoon of the olive oil, the green and black olives and chop coarsely. Add the mayonnaise and mustard and blend to mix. Refrigerate until ready to serve.

To make the sandwich: Heat 1 tablespoon of the olive oil in a large, non-stick skillet over medium-high heat. When the oil is hot, add the tuna steaks and sear one side quickly. Turn over and reduce heat; cook 3 to 4 minutes on second side. Tuna should feel firm to the touch when pressed with your fingertips. Remove fish from skillet.

Spread the slices of bread with the olive mixture. Sandwich the tuna and sliced tomato between the bread. Slice crosswise into 4 wedges. Using 1 tablespoon of the remaining olive oil per side, toast the sandwich wedges in the same skillet or on a griddle. Regulate the heat to keep the bread from burning. Serve warm with extra olive relish.

Makes 4 servings.

Note: Make individual sandwiches on slices of crusty French bread or on English muffins.

Look for the tail end of a salmon fillet for this delicate sandwich. The tail portion is the thinnest section and perfect for sandwiches.

Grilled Salmon and Artichoke Sandwich

3/4 pound salmon fillet, sliced about 1/4 inch thick
1 (6-ounce) jar marinated artichoke hearts, drained (reserve marinade)
4 slices challah or egg bread, large enough to hold the fish
3 tablespoons butter or margarine

 orange roughy, tuna, flounder, catfish

Remove the skin from the salmon. Cut fish into two pieces about the size of the bread.

Place the fish in a microwave-safe baking dish, thickest pieces toward the outside. Drizzle with 1 tablespoon of the artichoke marinade. Cover loosely with plastic wrap or wax paper. Cook on high (100 percent) power for 2 minutes; rotate dish and cook on high (100 percent) power for 2 minutes longer. Salmon should be firm to the touch and dotted with white-colored beads of cooking moisture. Allow to stand 3 minutes at room temperature.

In a blender or a food processor, puree the drained artichokes with 1 tablespoon of reserved marinade. Spread the artichoke puree on the challah or egg bread. Sandwich the salmon in between. Melt half the butter in a skillet over medium heat and toast one side until the bread is golden and crusty. Add remaining butter and toast the second side.

Makes 2 sandwiches.

Note: Challah is a traditional Jewish yeast bread with a light texture and golden color. It's similar to French brioche but is usually sold as a long braided loaf.

Smoked Fish Hero

Smoked Fish Pate (recipe page 10)
1 head butter or Boston lettuce
1 cucumber, peeled and thinly sliced
4 sourdough sandwich rolls or 8 slices light rye bread

Spread the bread with the Smoked Fish Pate. Layer with the lettuce and cucumber. Serve chilled.

Makes 4 sandwiches.

Notes: The Smoked Fish Pate can be made several days in advance and stored in the refrigerator. You should have enough for 6 sandwiches.

Fresh Tuna Salad Sandwiches

3/4 pound fresh tuna, sliced about 1/2 inch thick
2 teaspoons lemon or lime juice
3 tablespoons mayonnaise
1 1/2 tablespoons whole-grain mustard
2 tablespoons sweet pickle relish
1/2 Golden Delicious apple, very finely diced (about 1/2 cup)
Salt and pepper to taste

Grill extra tuna and chill the leftovers to make awesome tuna salad sandwiches the next day. This recipe is excellent made with Garlicky Grilled Tuna (page 73), Tuna Teriyaki (Page 70) or Grilled Tuna and Vegetables with Orange Vinaigrette (Page 57).

Sprinkle the tuna with the fresh lemon or lime juice. Arrange in a microwave-safe baking dish. Cover loosely with plastic wrap or wax paper. Cook on high (100 percent) power for 2 minutes. Turn dish and cook for 2 minutes longer, until meat is grayish white. Allow fish to cool to room temperature.

Chop the tuna into small pieces. Mix with mayonnaise, mustard, pickle relish and apple.

Serve on toasted rye or whole wheat bread with lettuce and tomato. Sandwiches are excellent when spread with Creamy Dill Topping (recipe page 207)

Makes 2 cups or enough for 4 sandwiches.

For a quick lunch or summer dinner, nothing beats these nutritious, California-style rolled sandwiches.

Chilled Crab, Avocado and Sprout Burritos

12 ounces imitation crab, flaked

1 medium ripe California avocado, peeled, pitted and diced

2 tablespoons lime juice

1 stalk celery, diced

1/2 cucumber, peeled, seeded and diced

2 tablespoons mayonnaise

2 tablespoons plain low-fat yogurt

1 teaspoon horseradish

1 teaspoon whole-grain mustard

1/2 cup commercial salsa, mild, medium or hot

1 1/2 cups alfalfa sprouts

6 large flour tortillas

In a bowl combine the imitation crab meat, avocado, lime juice, celery and cucumber. Stir in the mayonnaise, yogurt, horseradish, mustard and salsa. Toss well to combine. Divide the salad into 6 even portions and spoon down the center of each tortilla. Top with sprouts and roll up. Place seam-side down on plates or secure with toothpicks.

Makes 6 servings.

crab meat, cooked baby shrimp

Make the imitation crab salad up to 3 days in advance and assemble the burritos when ready to serve.

Eat these creamy, good sandwiches with a fork. Muenster cheese becomes very runny as it melts but it browns wonderfully. Monterey Jack is less runny and soft but doesn't brown quite as well.

Crab and Green Chili Melts

12 ounces imitation crab meat, flaked
1 ripe tomato, seeded and diced
2 green onions, finely chopped
1 (4-ounce) can diced green chilis, hot or mild
8 black olives, sliced into rounds
2 tablespoons mayonnaise
1/4 teaspoon salt
1/4 teaspoon black pepper
1/4 teaspoon ground cumin
4 ounces Muenster or Monterey Jack cheese, shredded
4 English muffins, split in halves

In a small bowl, combine the imitation crab meat, tomato, green onions, green chili and olives. Stir in the mayonnaise, salt, pepper and cumin. Toss well to combine. Pile on English muffin halves and top with shredded Muenster cheese.

Preheat oven broiler. Broil about 4 inches from heat for 3 to 4 minutes, until cheese is brown and bubbly.

Makes 4 servings.

 crab meat, cooked baby shrimp, canned tuna

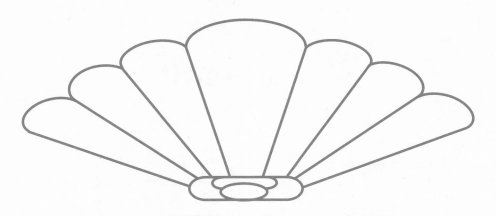

CANNED FISH

A simple can of salmon can turn breakfast into an elegant brunch or a weekday dinner into a special occasion.

Seattle Souffle

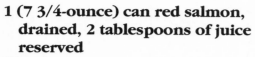

1 (7 3/4-ounce) can red salmon, drained, 2 tablespoons of juice reserved
6 eggs
1/2 teaspoon salt
1/2 teaspoon dill
1/4 teaspoon white pepper
1/8 teaspoon nutmeg
2 teaspoons olive oil
1/4 cup grated Parmesan cheese

 cooked fresh salmon, canned tuna, clams or crab

Preheat oven to 375 F.

Pick through the salmon, discarding any skin and bones. Break the meat into chunks. Set aside.

Separate 4 of the eggs. In a large bowl combine the 2 whole eggs and 4 egg yolks. Add the reserved liquid from the can, the salt, white pepper, dill and nutmeg. Beat with a whisk until no streaks of yolk remain visible. Stir in the salmon. Set aside.

With an electric mixer, beat the 4 egg whites on medium speed until they form soft peaks. Increase power and continue beating whites until they hold stiff peaks and don't slide when the bowl is tipped.

Using a rubber spatula, fold the whites into the yolk mixture by thirds, being careful not to overbeat.

Heat the olive oil in a heavy, ovenproof skillet. Swirl it around so the oil coats the bottom and sides. Pour in the souffle mixture and sprinkle the Parmesan cheese on top. Cook on medium-high heat for 2 minutes until the bottom is set. Place in the preheated oven and bake for 10 to 12 minutes, until the souffle is golden and the center is firm. Serve immediately. The souffle will fall when removed from the oven.

Makes 6 servings.

A frittata is nothing more than an Italian omelet that has all the ingredients mixed with the eggs rather than folded inside. Browning the top under the broiler cuts cooking time to a few minutes.

Spinach, Salmon and Raisin Frittata

1 (6-ounce) can skinless, boneless salmon
1 tablespoon olive oil
1 tablespoon butter
2 green onions, finely chopped
1/3 cup raisins, plumped in warm water for 10 minutes and drained
2 ounces fresh spinach, washed and drained (about 1 large handful or 2 cups packed)
4 eggs lightly beaten
1/4 teaspoon salt
1/4 teaspoon pepper
Pinch nutmeg

Drain the salmon and place near the stove.

In a bowl, combine the eggs, salt, pepper and nutmeg. Beat lightly to combine well. Place near the stove.

In a large, non-stick skillet, heat the oil and butter. When the butter starts to foam, add the green onions and raisins. Cook for 3 minutes, until soft. Add the spinach and stir until it wilts. Pour the eggs over the vegetables. Sprinkle the salmon on top. Reduce heat to medium low; cook for 5 minutes.

Preheat the oven broiler. Cook the frittata about 4 inches from the heat element for 4 to 5 minutes, until the egg mixture is brown on top and the center is set. The eggs should be slightly moist in the center. Allow to stand a few minutes before slicing into wedges.

Makes 4 to 5 servings.

This delectable blend has all the ingredients of a faux salad Nicoise – tuna, green beans and a good vinaigrette dressing.

Tuna Potato Salad

8 medium red-skinned potatoes
1 (6 1/2-ounce) can tuna, packed in water
2 cups cooked green beans, fresh, frozen-and-thawed or canned
1 green onion, chopped
1/4 cup chopped fresh parsley
1 cup green peas, frozen and thawed
1/2 cup Garlic Tarragon Vinaigrette (recipe page 36) or Sara's Honey-Balsamic Vinegar Dressing and Marinade (recipe page 197)

Scrub the potatoes thoroughly under running water. Do not peel. Prick with a knife or fork. Cook on high (100 percent) power in a microwave oven for 18 to 20 minutes or until soft. Allow to stand for 10 minutes at room temperature.

Drain the tuna and combine in a large mixing bowl with the beans, onion, parsley and peas. Cube the hot potatoes and add them to the bowl. Pour the dressing over and toss to combine. Taste for salt and pepper.

Serve chilled or at room temperature. Makes 8 servings.

Notes: If you have an herb garden, throw in some chopped basil, thyme or oregano.

This is a great way to "doctor" canned products to make them taste freshly made.

Lightning White Clam Sauce

1 tablespoon olive oil
2 green onions, chopped
1 clove garlic, crushed through a press
1 (10 1/2-ounce) can or (12-ounce) jar
    white clam sauce
1 (6 1/2-ounce) can chopped clams
3 tablespoons white wine
3 tablespoons chopped fresh parsley
1/4 cup freshly grated Parmesan or
    Romano cheese
Cooked pasta or rice

Heat the oil in a non-stick skillet and saute the green onion until limp, about 3 to 4 minutes. Add the garlic and cook for 1 minute longer. Add the canned clam sauce, the chopped baby clams, wine and parsley. Bring to a boil and simmer for 2 to 3 minutes. Serve hot over pasta, such as linguine, fettuccine, angel hair or rigatoni. Sprinkle cheese on top of pasta.
Makes 4 servings.

Make the sauce in advance and store it in batches in the freezer. Thaw it in the microwave oven for an instant dinner.

Fish Favorites

The following varieties are the most popular in the United States:

1. Tuna (consumed mostly as canned tuna)
2. Shrimp
3. Cod
4. Alaskan pollock (consumed mostly as surimi or imitation crab)
5. Salmon
6. Catfish
7. Clams
8. Flounder or sole
9. Scallops
10. Crab meat

SOURCE: National Fisheries Institute

Mustard, lemon and dill give these easy "burgers" special appeal. Serve with Old Fashioned Tartar Sauce (recipe page 200).

Tuna Burgers

—◆—

2 (6 1/2-ounce) cans tuna, packed in
  water
3/4 cup fresh, soft bread crumbs
1 green onion, finely chopped
2 tablespoons finely chopped celery
2 eggs
2 tablespoons Dijon-style mustard
2 tablespoons fresh lemon or lime
  juice
1/2 teaspoon dill
1/2 teaspoon basil or oregano
3 tablespoons canola or peanut oil for
  frying

Drain the tuna. In a mixing bowl, combine tuna, bread crumbs, onion, celery, eggs, mustard, lemon juice and herbs. Mix well and form into patties. Heat the oil in a non-stick skillet or on a griddle. Fry the patties for 6 minutes per side, or until golden brown. Turn gently.

If desired, serve on toasted hamburger buns with tomato slices, lettuce and a sauce.

Makes 6 burgers.

Notes: This mixture can also be made into 1-inch balls for appetizers. Cook in a skillet as directed or bake on lightly oiled baking sheets until golden brown.

The hot and cold effect of these sandwiches is part of their appeal. You can also cut them in wedges or slices to serve for appetizers.

Norwegian Broiled Sardine Sandwiches

—◆—

4 slices thin pumpernickel or light rye
  bread
2 tablespoons mayonnaise
1 tablespoon Dijon-style mustard
2 ounces thinly sliced Jarlsberg or
  other Swiss cheese
1 (3 3/4-ounce) can sardines
1/2 red onion, sliced paper thin
1/2 cucumber, sliced paper thin

Combine the mayonnaise and the mustard. Spread the bread with a thin coating of the mixture. Top with cheese, red onion and sardines.

Heat the oven broiler and toast the sandwiches until the cheese is melted and the sardines begin to blister.

Remove from heat and top with thin slices of cucumber.

Makes 4 sandwiches.

Lavosh are round flat breads, which resemble oversized flour tortillas. They're certainly a great way to make a rolled tuna sandwich. If you cannot find lavosh, substitute large flour tortillas made with all-vegetable shortening.

Lavosh Rollups

2 circles of lavosh (15-16 inches in diameter)

1 (6 1/2-ounce) can light tuna, packed in water

2 stalks celery, finely diced (about 1/3 cup)

1 green onion, finely chopped

1/2 teaspoon dried tarragon or 2 tablespoons fresh tarragon, finely chopped

2 tablespoons commercial fat-free ranch dressing

1 medium tomato, thinly sliced

4 leaves lettuce, whole or shredded

Drain tuna and discard water. Combine tuna, celery, green onion, tarragon and ranch dressing. Stir well to blend.

Spread the filling evenly over the entire circle of lavosh, including the edges. Top with thinly sliced tomato, shredded lettuce or other desired topping. Roll up like a pinwheel and slice crosswise into 4 sections.

Serve cool or at room temperature.

Makes 4 servings or 12 appetizer portions.

Notes: You can also layer slices of Swiss or Havarti cheese in this rolled sandwich. Make the sandwich in advance by rolling it and covering it with damp paper towels until ready to serve.

This salty, robustly flavored spread hails from the sunny Provence region of Southern France. It makes a wonderful appetizer with red wine, cheese and apples. It's also great to take on picnics and ski trips.

Tapenade

1 (6 3/4-ounce) can tuna, packed in water

1 (2-ounce) can anchovies, packed in olive oil

1 cup pitted black olives

1 tablespoon capers, drained

2 tablespoons olive oil

3 tablespoons mayonnaise

1 tablespoon lemon juice

4 tablespoons finely minced fresh parsley

 Make the dip up to 1 week in advance. Store in a crock with a tight-fitting lid.

Drain the tuna and anchovies thoroughly. Combine the tuna, anchovies, black olives and capers in a food processor or blender. Process until olives are chopped into bits. Add the olive oil, mayonnaise, lemon juice and parsley. Turn machine on and off, long enough to blend ingredients but not puree them. It should be slightly chunky. Refrigerate until ready to serve.

Serve with French bread, apples, celery or cucumber slices.

Makes 1 cup.

The longer this spread sits, the more flavor it develops.

Sardine Pate

1 (3 3/4-ounce) can sardines in oil,
  drained
1 (8-ounce) package cream cheese
1 tablespoon mayonnaise
1 tablespoon Dijon-style mustard
1 tablespoon lemon juice
1 tablespoon minced fresh parsley
Sliced cucumbers, for decoration

Break the sardines up with a fork into small pieces. Set aside.

In the bowl of a food processor or an electric mixer, beat the cream cheese until soft. Add the mayonnaise, mustard and lemon juice. Beat until soft. Fold in the sardines and parsley.

Line a 2-cup bowl or mold with plastic wrap. Pack in the sardine pate, smoothing top. Cover with another sheet of plastic wrap and allow to chill several hours or overnight. Unmold and peel away plastic wrap. Smooth surface with the smooth blade of a knife. If desired, decorate with slices of cucumber. Serve with French bread, crackers or triangles of sliced, toasted bread.

Makes 1 1/2 cups or 24 servings.

EXTRAS

Red Pepper Mayonnaise

1 red bell pepper, roasted and peeled
   or 1 (4-ounce) jar pimentos
1 cup mayonnaise
1/4 teaspoon sugar
1 clove garlic, peeled
2 tablespoons red wine vinegar
Pinch salt

In a blender or food processor, combine the red bell pepper or pimento and the garlic. Puree. Add the mayonnaise, sugar, vinegar and salt. Puree to make a smooth sauce.

Serve chilled with cooked fish, shrimp, scallops or other shellfish.

Makes 1 1/2 cups.

Notes: You can also make this using Red Pepper Puree (recipe page 210).

Cocktail Sauce

1/2 cup commercial chili sauce
3 tablespoons ketchup
1 tablespoon finely chopped yellow
   onion
1 tablespoon prepared horseradish
1 tablespoon lemon juice
1 teaspoon Worcestershire sauce

Combine all ingredients in a bowl and stir well to blend. Refrigerate and allow flavors to blend.

Makes 2/3 cup.

A gift from my aunt Sara Balcomb

Sara's Honey-Balsamic Vinegar Dressing and Marinade

3 tablespoons balsamic vinegar
2 tablespoons raspberry vinegar
2/3 cup olive oil
Juice of 1/2 lemon or 1 1/2
 tablespoons prepared juice
3 cloves of garlic, crushed through a
 press
1 tablespoon Dijon mustard
1 tablespoon honey

Shake well to blend. Store in refrigerator. Warm to room temperature before serving.

Makes 1 cup.

Awesome when spooned over grilled, baked or steamed fish! The colorful, slightly spicy salsa is great for people watching their weight because it adds incredible flavor but no calories from fat.

Mango Salsa

2 small ripe mangoes or 1 large mango (about 1 1/2 cups peeled and cubed)

1/2 red bell pepper, diced (about 1/2 cup)

1/2 green bell pepper, diced (about 1/2 cup)

1/2 jalapeno pepper, seeded and finely diced (about 2 teaspoons)

1 small purple onion, diced (about 1/2 cup)

1 clove garlic, crushed through a press

4 tablespoons pineapple juice

2 tablespoons lime juice

2 tablespoons white wine vinegar

4 tablespoons chopped fresh cilantro

1 teaspoon curry powder

1/2 teaspoon sugar

1/4 teaspoon salt

4 dashes liquid hot sauce

Peel mango and slice lengthwise on either side of the big central pit. Use a paring knife to cut the rest of the fruit off the pit. Discard the pit and cube the fruit.

Combine the mango, red and green pepper, jalapeno pepper, onion and garlic. Add the remaining ingredients and toss well to combine. Allow flavors to blend at least 15 minutes before serving. Salsa can also be made up to two days in advance.

Serve with grilled, baked or microwave-cooked fish.

Makes about 2 1/2 cups.

Notes: Some people have an allergic reaction to the skin – not the fruit – of the mango. People who have sensitive skin or who suffer from hives or rashes, may experience redness, swelling and itching from handling a mango. One alternative to fresh mango are the slices frequently sold in the refrigerated section of the grocery store or canned mango. Canned mango comes in heavy syrup, so increase the amount of lime juice or vinegar to counteract the sweetness.

Pungent and lemon-colored, this has innumerable uses as a spread, a dip or a salad dressing.

Curried Mayonnaise

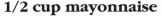

1 cup mayonnaise
1 teaspoon lemon juice
2 teaspoons curry powder
1/4 teaspoon cumin powder
1/4 teaspoon cardamom
1/4 teaspoon paprika
1/4 teaspoon sugar

In a small bowl, combine all the ingredients. Stir well. Refrigerate for 15 to 20 minutes or overnight to allow the flavors to blend. Use as a dip for steamed shrimp or a condiment instead of cole slaw for Fish Dogs (recipe page 177).
Makes 1 cup.

Notes: If you like a milder flavor, cut the curry powder down to 1 teaspoon. Add a little cayenne pepper if you like it spicy.

My friend Louise Cutting, who is an extraordinary hostess, serves a similar version of this Tarragon Cream Sauce with foil-steamed salmon at her annual Christmas party. Let it sit overnight so the flavors can develop.

Tarragon Cream Sauce

1/2 cup mayonnaise
1/2 cup yogurt
1/2 teaspoon sugar
1 teaspoon dry mustard
1 heaping teaspoon dried tarragon
1 teaspoon minced fresh parsley

Combine all ingredients and refrigerate. Allow flavors to blend several hours or overnight. Serve with chilled fish.
Makes 1 1/4 cups.

Incredibly good and ridiculously easy.

Honey Mustard Sauce

2 tablespoons Dijon-style mustard
2 tablespoons mayonnaise
1 tablespoon honey
1 tablespoon red wine vinegar

Combine all ingredients in a jar with a tight-fitting lid. Allow flavors to blend in the refrigerator. Serve with crab cakes, steamed shrimp or grilled fish. Especially good with amberjack.

Makes 1/2 cup.

There is so much commercial sauce on the market, few Americans ever taste the real thing. This is wonderfully fresh and light.

Old Fashioned Tartar Sauce

1/4 cup mayonnaise
1/3 cup reduced-calorie sour cream
1 hard-boiled egg, peeled and finely chopped
1 green onion, minced
2 tablespoons sweet pickle relish
1 tablespoon capers, drained and finely chopped
2 teaspoons cider vinegar
Few drops hot sauce

In a mixing bowl, combine all the ingredients and stir well to mix. Allow flavors to blend in the refrigerator a few minutes before serving.

Use with baked or fried fish.

Makes 1 scant cup.

These delectable pancakes are good with just about any seafood dish. They can be made in advance and frozen.

Fresh Corn Pancakes

3/4 cup yellow cornmeal
1/2 cup all-purpose flour
1/2 teapoon baking powder
1 teaspoon salt
1/2 teaspoon sugar
1/2 teaspoon dried parsley, crushed
   or 1 tablespoon finely chopped
   fresh parsley
1 1/4 cups buttermilk
2 egg whites
1 egg yolk
2 tablespoons corn oil
1 cup corn kernels, divided
1 green onion (optional)

In a large bowl, combine the flour, cornmeal, baking powder, salt, sugar and parsley. Stir to combine.

In a separate bowl, combine the buttermilk, egg whites, egg yolk, oil and 1/2 cup of the corn kernels. Stir to blend. In a blender or food processor, combine remaining 1/2 cup corn and optional green onion. Puree to make a smooth paste.

Stir the pureed mixture into the buttermilk, eggs and oil. Stir the liquid ingredients into the dry ingredients until mixture is soupy, about the consistency of heavy cream. (If mixture is too stiff, thin with a few additional drops of buttermilk.)

Cook pancakes over medium heat on a non-stick griddle. Serve with hot pepper jelly, if desired.

Makes 33 2-inch pancakes.

Notes: In season, use fresh corn to make these light pancakes. To remove the kernels, cut down the ears with a sharp knife. Then, turn the knife over and scrape with the dull side of the blade to get the tender germ inside. Frozen, thawed corn or canned corn will also work.

Buttered Croutons

1/2 loaf day-old French or Italian bread
4 tablespoons butter
4 tablespoons olive oil

Preheat oven to 325 F.

Slice the bread into 1/2-inch pieces. Cut the slices into 1-inch cubes. In a microwave-safe dish, melt the butter and the olive oil. Drizzle the olive oil and butter over the bread, tossing to coat all sides lightly.

Bake for 10 to 12 minutes, until croutons are crusty and lightly golden brown.

Add to soups and Caesar salads.

Makes 6 servings.

Notes: For a garlicky flavor, add 1 clove of garlic, crushed through a press or 1/4 teaspoon garlic powder to the butter and oil mixture before drizzling it over bread. Onion powder also adds a nice flavor.

Brush this fine-flavored oil on grilled fish, bread or pizza crusts, or use it to saute vegetables. Be sure to store it in the refrigerator. It will add flavor to food for several months.

Roasted Garlic Oil

1 cup canola or peanut oil
5 cloves garlic, peeled

Place the oil and the garlic in a saucepan over medium heat. Cook until the garlic starts to fry in the oil and turns golden brown. Turn off heat and allow garlic and oil to cool to room temperature. Pour into a clean jar or bottle with an air-tight lid. Store in the refrigerator.
Makes 1 cup.

 Use this versatile sauce for pasta or as a topping for baked or microwave-cooked fish.

Low-Fat Creamy White Sauce

1 tablespoon olive oil
2 tablespoons flour
1/4 teaspoon white pepper
1/8 teaspoon nutmeg
1 (12-ounce) can evaporated skim milk
3 tablespoons white wine or vermouth
3 tablespoons low-fat cream cheese

Heat the oil in a small saucepan. Combine the flour, white pepper and nutmeg in a small dish. Whisk the flour into the oil. Cook over medium heat for 1 minute. Whisk in the evaporated skim milk and cook until the mixture comes to a boil. Cook for 2 minutes. Add the white wine or vermouth and the cream cheese. Whisk until the cream cheese has melted.
Makes 2 1/4 cups.

Notes: There are no limits on the number of variations on this sauce. For example, add basil or tarragon for an herbed white sauce; add garlic, sauteed onions or mushrooms for a robust white sauce. You can also substitute dry sherry for the white wine or vermouth. Stir in a little grated Parmesan cheese or shredded Swiss cheese. When baked, this sauce forms a golden-brown crust.

Light and spicy, just like chefs make it in the fancy resorts of Acapulco and Cancun, Mexico.

Mexican Lime Marinade

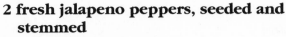

2 fresh jalapeno peppers, seeded and stemmed
2 cloves garlic, peeled
1/4 cup white wine vinegar
4 tablespoons freshly squeezed lime juice
2 tablespoons olive oil
1/4 teaspoon ground cumin
1/4 teaspoon salt
1/4 teaspoon pepper
1/4 teaspoon sugar

Place the peppers and garlic in a blender or food processor. Process until both are finely chopped. Add the white wine vinegar, olive oil, cumin, salt, pepper and sugar and puree. Pour over fish and allow to marinate for 30 minutes to an hour.

Use with cod, red snapper, sea bass, halibut, grouper or tuna.

Makes 1/2 cup.

 A fine, light marinade that forms a delectable coating on fish as it cooks. This is exceptional on fresh kingfish steaks.

Garlic Yogurt Marinade for Grilled Fish

1/4 cup canola oil
2 tablespoons lemon juice
2 cloves garlic, peeled
1/4 cup chopped fresh parsley
1/2 teaspoon dried basil or 4 table-spoons fresh basil leaves
1/2 teaspoon dried tarragon or 4 tablespoons fresh tarragon
1 (8-ounce) carton plain low-fat or non-fat yogurt

Combine all ingredients in a blender or food processor. Puree to make a smooth mixture. Pour over fish and allow to marinate 30 minutes to 1 hour.

Brush marinade over fish while grilling. Cook over medium-high heat. Discard any remaining marinade. Use on kingfish, tuna, swordfish, salmon, cod, grouper, red snapper or dolphin.

Makes 3/4 cup.

Russian Dill Dressing

1/4 cup canola oil
3 tablespoons rice vinegar or cider vinegar
3 tablespoons ketchup
1/2 teaspoon sugar
1/2 teaspoon Worcestershire sauce
1 teaspoon dill
1 teaspoon Dijon-style mustard
Pinch salt and white pepper

In a jar with a tight-fitting lid, combine all the ingredients and shake vigorously. Shake well and taste before using.

Use as a dressing for salads topped with cooked seafood or as a dip for croquettes or fish sticks.

Makes 2/3 cup.

Blender Bearnaise

1/4 cup tarragon vinegar
1/4 cup dry white wine or vermouth
1 shallot, peeled and finely chopped
1/2 teaspoon dried tarragon
1/8 teaspoon black pepper
2 tablespoons finely chopped fresh tarragon or parsley
3 egg yolks
1/4 teaspoon salt
1 tablespoon lemon juice
1/2 cup unsalted butter

In a small saucepan or a microwave-safe container, combine the tarragon vinegar, wine, shallot, black pepper, tarragon and the fresh tarragon or parsley. Bring mixture to a boil and cook on high heat or in a microwave at 100 percent power for a few minutes until the liquid is reduced by half. Strain the mixture into a fine sieve, pressing to remove all the liquid possible. Discard the solids.

Pour the liquid into a blender or food processor. With the machine running, add the egg yolks, salt and lemon juice.

Melt the butter in a saucepan or in a microwave oven until it is bubbling. Turn on the blender or food processor and pour the hot butter in a thin stream with the machine running. Mixture should thicken to the consistency of sour cream.

Serve over baked fish or with fish cooked en papillote. Also excellent with grilled or broiled salmon, halibut or tuna.

Makes 2/3 cup.

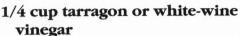

This low-fat alternative is just as creamy and tasty as the traditional bearnaise sauce. It's made with one egg yolk, a touch of cornstarch, chicken broth and cream.

Butterless Bearnaise

1/4 cup tarragon or white-wine
    vinegar
1/4 cup white wine or vermouth
2 tablespoons onions or green onions,
    finely minced
2 teaspoons dried tarragon or 1
    tablespoon fresh
1/8 teaspoon white pepper
1/8 teaspoon salt
1 egg yolk
2 teaspoons cornstarch
2 tablespoons chicken broth
3 tablespoons heavy cream

In a small saucepan, combine the 1/4 cup wine vinegar, 1/4 cup white wine, minced onions, tarragon and white pepper.

Bring the vinegar mixture to a rolling boil over high heat. Cook for about 10 minutes, until the mixture is reduced by half. Strain mixture through a fine sieve into a small dish.

After straining, there should be about 1/4 cup liquid. Rinse out the saucepan. Whisk together the egg yolk, 1/8 teaspoon salt, 2 teaspoons cornstarch and 2 tablespoons chicken broth.

Stir a spoonful of the hot vinegar-tarragon mixture in to warm the egg mixture, then whisk in the remaining vinegar-tarragon mixture.

Place the saucepan over very low heat and cook, stirring constantly, until the sauce thickens. This should only take about 3 to 5 minutes. Whisk in cream and remove from heat.

Serve hot over grilled or baked fish, crab, shrimp or broiled oysters.

Makes 1/2 cup.

Make-Your-Own Ranch Dressing

2 cloves garlic, peeled
1 cup plain low-fat yogurt
1/2 cup salad oil
4 tablespoons lemon juice
4 tablespoons chopped parsley
2 teaspoons dried minced onion or 3
    tablespoons fresh onion
1/2 teaspoon dried oregano
1/2 teaspoon dried basil
1/2 teaspoon dried rosemary leaves
1/2 teaspoon salt
1/2 teaspoon sugar
1/2 teaspoon black pepper

Combine all ingredients in a blender or food processor. Puree until mixture is smooth. Store in refrigerator.

Serve over salads topped with seafood or as a dip for steamed shrimp or mussels.

Makes 1 1/2 cups.

Creamy Dill Topping for Broiled Fish

1/3 cup mayonnaise
1 tablespoon lemon juice
1 tablespoon honey
1 tablespoon cider vinegar
2 tablespoons fresh minced dill or 1
    teaspoon dried dill

In a small bowl, combine all the ingredients. Spoon over fish fillets. Broil in the oven about 4 inches from the heat until the fish is firm to the touch and the topping is lightly browned.

Makes 2/3 cup.

In summertime, use fresh herbs for maximum flavor.

Citrus Marinade
for Grilled, Baked or Broiled Fish

2 tablespoons soy sauce
2 tablespoons orange juice, fresh or
reconstituted
1 tablespoon olive oil
1/2 teaspoon lemon zest (grated
yellow part of the peel)
1 tablespoon lemon juice
2 tablespoons tomato paste
1 clove garlic, crushed through a press
1/2 teaspoon dried basil or 2
tablespoons fresh chopped basil
1/2 teaspoon dried oregano or 2
tablespoons fresh chopped oregano

Combine all ingredients in a shallow dish. Stir well. Place fish in dish and allow to marinate in refrigerator for 1 hour.

Baste fish frequently with marinade while cooking.

Use with tuna, salmon, mahi mahi, swordfish, amberjack or shellfish.

Makes 1/2 cup.

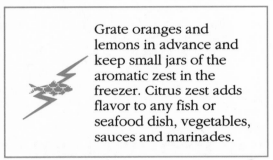

Grate oranges and lemons in advance and keep small jars of the aromatic zest in the freezer. Citrus zest adds flavor to any fish or seafood dish, vegetables, sauces and marinades.

Ginger, Molasses and Mustard Marinade for Grilled Fish

1/4 cup lemon juice
2 tablespoons soy sauce
1 tablespoon molasses
1 teaspoon fresh grated or minced
   ginger
1 tablespoon Dijon-style mustard

 To keep fresh ginger indefinitely, finely mince it or grind it in a food processor. Submerge in dry sherry or rice wine. Store it in the refrigerator in a small jar.

Combine all ingredients, stirring well to mix molasses. Pour over fish and marinate for 1 hour. Grill fish over medium-high heat, basting frequently while cooking. Do not allow fish to scorch, as molasses burns when exposed to flame.

Use with salmon, tuna, mahi mahi, amberjack, squid or shrimp.

Makes 1/2 cup.

Easy Herb Dip for Shellfish

1/2 cup commercial oil-and-vinegar
   dressing
3 tablespoons mayonnaise
2 tablespoons whole-grain or Dijon-
   style mustard
1/2 teaspoon salad-herb blend or basil
1 green onion, finely chopped
1 teaspoon lemon juice

Combine all ingredients in a small bowl. Stir to combine. Refrigerate for at least 10 to 15 minutes before serving to allow flavors to mix.

Makes 1 cup.

This all-purpose sauce will make any fast weekday dinner taste like a caterer showed up to prepare it. Freeze the sauce in quarter-cup containers and thaw it in a microwave oven. Use with broiled, grilled, baked or steamed fish. It's also excellent cooked with the fish en papillote.

Red Pepper Puree

2 large red bell peppers
1 tablespoon olive oil
1 tablespoon balsamic vinegar
1/4 teaspoon sugar
Pinch salt

Roast the peppers according to one of the following methods. Puree the roasted peppers with the olive oil, balsamic vinegar, salt and sugar. Use immediately or freeze in convenient containers until later.

Roasting in the oven: Preheat the broiler. Slice the peppers in half lengthwise. Broil, skin-side up for 3 to 5 minutes, until the skin blackens and blisters. Place in a heavy plastic bag or a deep container with a tight-fitting lid. Allow to steam for 15 to 20 minutes. Peel and discard skin, seeds and stems. Reserve flesh and any juices.

On a grill: Roast over medium-high heat, turning frequently until the skin is charred and blistered. Place in a heavy plastic bag or a deep container with a tight-fitting lid. Allow to steam for 15 to 20 minutes. Peel and discard skin, seeds and stems. Reserve flesh and any juices.

In a microwave oven: Remove seeds and stems. Cut into large pieces. Place in a microwave-safe container or heavy plastic bag. Cook on high (100 percent) power for 6 to 7 minutes, until the peppers are wilted and watery. Allow to stand a few minutes.

Makes 1 1/4 cups.

Make this garlic-scented bread to serve when you are making a dinner of grilled fish or shellfish.

Grill-Toasted Garlic Bread

1 loaf French, Italian or sourdough bread, cut into 1-inch slices
3 tablespoons olive oil
2 tablespoons mayonnaise
2 cloves garlic, crushed through a press

Combine the olive oil, mayonnaise and garlic and stir to make a thick liquid. Brush lightly over both sides of the sliced bread. Grill on the back part or outside of the grill away from the direct heat of the coals. Grill until bread is crusty but not dried out and surfaces are toasty brown. If any oil mixture remains, brush again lightly just before removing from heat.

Makes 6 to 8 servings.

MAKE AHEAD

This dish of marinated, pickled fish is famous in South America and in Spain. Serve it for tapas, those delicious Spanish-style afternoon snacks. Do not confuse escabeche (es-cah-BAY-chay) with seviche (say-VEE-chay). Seviche, which is Mexican in origin, is a spicy salad made from raw fish or scallops that have been marinated in lime juice and hot peppers.

Pescado en Escabeche (Marinated Fish)

1 pound medium-firm or firm fish
1 tablespoon flour
1/4 teaspoon salt
4 tablespoons olive oil
2 cloves garlic, crushed through a
    press
1 small red onion, halved and thinly
    sliced (about 1 cup)
1/2 green pepper, sliced into strips
1/2 red pepper, sliced into strips
1 small carrot, sliced into thin rounds
1 bay leaf
1/4 teaspoon thyme leaves
1/4 teaspoon black pepper
8 green olives, pitted and sliced in half
1 teaspoon paprika
2 teaspoons sugar
1/4 cup white-wine vinegar
1/4 cup dry white wine
1/2 cup bottled clam juice

kingfish, grouper, tuna,
mackerel, bluefish,
sole, orange roughy

Remove bones from fish, if any. Cut into large pieces. Combine flour and salt on a plate and dust each piece lightly on both sides with mixture.

Heat 1 tablespoon olive oil in a large, non-stick skillet until it is hot. Add the fish and cook quickly until flour browns, about 5 minutes. Turn and cook on other side, about 4 minutes. Remove from heat, leaving as much oil as possible in the skillet. Arrange the fish in a flat glass or ceramic dish.

Add the remaining oil to the skillet. Cook garlic, sliced onions, sliced green and red pepper, carrot, herbs and bay leaf over medium-high heat until vegetables are crisp tender, about 7 minutes. Stir in the olives, paprika, sugar, vinegar, wine and clam juice. Bring liquids to a boil and continue to stir. Cover and cook 2 to 3 minutes longer. Remove from heat.

Pour the vegetable mixture and liquids over the fish. Fish should be submerged in liquid. Refrigerate for 3 hours or overnight.

Serve chilled, with lettuce and crusty Cuban bread, if desired.

Makes 8 servings.

This is a light variation on heavy, traditional Eastern European recipes for stuffed cabbage. The cabbage leaves are filled with flavorful mousse of salmon and white-fish. Serve as a luncheon dish or as a first course for an elegant dinner party.

Salmon Stuffed Cabbage

1 medium head of savoy cabbage
  (about 1 1/2 pounds)
2 quarts boiling, salted water
1 pound fresh salmon
1/2 pound flaky fish, such as cod,
  haddock or flounder
2 egg whites
1/4 teaspoon salt
1/8 teaspoon white pepper
1/8 teaspoon nutmeg
1/8 teaspoon dill
2 tablespoons whipping cream
1/2 cup cooked rice
Tomato Lemon Coulis (recipe follows)

Core cabbage. Drop head into the boiling water and cook for 3 to 4 minutes, until outside leaves are soft. Remove 12 to 14 leaves without tearing. (If necessary, soften inner leaves by returning head to boiling water for a few minutes.) Reserve 3 cups of boiling water. Lay each leaf, inner side up, on a flat surface. Cut a V shape to remove tough base of stem. Set leaves aside to cool.

Remove skin and any bones from salmon. Reserve 1/4 pound of the fish and cut it into thin slices about 1 inch long. Set aside. Combine remaining salmon, flaky fish, egg whites, salt, pepper, nutmeg, dill and whipping cream in the bowl of a food processor. Puree until smooth. Fold in cooked rice and slices of salmon. Spoon 2 to 4 tablespoons of salmon filling in center of each cabbage leaf. Fold sides over filling and roll up loosely. Secure rolls with a toothpick.

Line a steaming rack with extra cabbage leaves. Pack salmon rolls closely in rack and steam covered over boiling water for 20 minutes. Cabbage should be tender and almost translucent; the filling should be firm to the touch.

Serve hot, surrounded by Tomato Lemon Coulis.

Makes 6 servings.

Notes: You can also bake the cabbage leaves: Preheat the oven to 375 degrees. Line a baking dish with extra cabbage leaves. Pack salmon rolls into dish and pour 1 to 1 1/2 cups of water over rolls. Cover dish with foil and bake for 30 minutes.

Tomato Lemon Coulis

1 strip lemon peel, about 1 inch long
1 tablespoon olive or canola oil
1 medium onion, chopped
1 teaspoon brown sugar
3 tomatoes, coarsely chopped
1/4 teaspoon salt
1/8 teaspoon pepper
1 tablespoon tomato ketchup
2 tablespoons fresh parsley, minced
1 teaspoon lemon juice

Using a vegetable peeler, remove the strip of yellow rind from the lemon. Avoid cutting into the bitter white pith. Chop rind finely.

Heat the oil in a saucepan. Add the chopped onion and lemon peel. Saute over medium-high heat until the onion is soft and transparent, about 5 to 6 minutes. Stir in the brown sugar and cook until it dissolves, about 1 minute.

Add the tomatoes, salt, pepper and ketchup. Reduce heat and cook for 10 minutes, until tomatoes are soft but not mushy. Stir in lemon juice and parsley. Put sauce in blender and puree.

Spoon around salmon rolls.

Makes 1 1/2 cups or 6 servings.

Passover Gefilte Fish Terrine

4 sole fillets, cut in half
Canola oil
2 medium onions, cut into 8 pieces
4 small carrots, peeled and sliced
1 stalk celery, sliced
1/4 cup chopped parsley
1 pound flaky white fish, cut into
 1-inch cubes
1 pound halibut, cut into 1-inch
 cubes
3 egg whites
1 whole egg
1/2 cup cold water
1/2 teaspoon salt
1/2 teaspoon white pepper
1 pound salmon fillet, cut into 1/2-
 inch cubes
Lettuce leaves
Sour Cream Horseradish Sauce
 (recipe follows)

 cod, orange roughy, lingcod, perch, flounder, turbot

Crisp sole by soaking it in cold saltwater for 15 minutes. Pat dry and cover with a sheet of waxed paper. Pound lightly with a coffee mug to flatten. Do not tear flesh.

Lightly oil a 2-quart baking dish or large glass loaf pan. Line with a sheet of parchment paper. Line the bottom and sides of the dish with sole fillets. Refrigerate while making filling. Combine the onion, carrots, celery and parsley in a food processor or blender and mince finely. Add the flaky white fish and halibut and process again. With the machine on, add the egg whites, water and whole egg. Add the salt and pepper.

Transfer the mixture to a large bowl. Fold in the salmon pieces. Pack the filling into the sole-lined mold. Cover with a sheet of oiled parchment paper. Cover with foil.

Preheat oven to 350 F. Place baking dish inside a larger pan of hot water. Bake for 50 minutes or until a knife inserted in the middle comes out clean. Cool for 10 minutes on a rack, then pour off excess liquid. Refrigerate at least 1 hour or overnight. Invert onto a serving platter and slice thinly into servings. Serve chilled on lettuce with a teaspoon of sauce on top.

Makes 12 servings.

Sour Cream Horseradish Sauce

1 (8-ounce) container fat-free sour
    cream substitute
2 tablespoons prepared horseradish

Combine the ingredients and stir well.
Refrigerate until serving.
    Makes 12 servings.

This oodles-of-stuff gumbo isn't all seafood but it makes a great party meal. Serve it over rice to absorb every drop of the sauce. It can be made in advance but don't add the shrimp and oysters until just before serving.

Louisiana-Style Gumbo

1/2 pound hot sausage, cut in 1-inch
    pieces
1/2 pound smoked sausage or
    andouille, cut in 1-inch pieces
1/2 pound boneless stew meat
4 tablespoons flour
1/2 cup canola or peanut oil, divided
1 large onion, chopped (about 1 cup)
2 quarts water
1/2 pound smoked ham, cubed
1 tablespoon paprika
1 teaspoon salt
3 cloves garlic, crushed through a
    press
1 teaspoon ground thyme
1/4 cup parsley, chopped
1 pound shrimp, shelled and deveined
1 pint shucked oysters with liquid
    reserved
Cooked rice

Cook the sausages and stew meat in 1/4 cup of the oil in a 6-quart pot over medium heat for about 15 minutes until done. Pour off fat. Set meat aside. Heat remaining oil in the kettle and add flour to make a roux. Stir constantly until very brown. Lower heat, add onion and cook over low heat until onions wilt.

Slowly stir in the water. Stir in the browned meats and ham, paprika, salt, garlic, parsley and thyme. Let simmer for 30 to 40 minutes.

About 10 minutes before serving, add shrimp and oysters and liquid. Cook for 10 minutes.

    Serve over rice.
    Makes 10 servings.

This dish blends the favorite flavors of Louisiana – seafood, onions, green peppers and tomatoes.

Creole-Style Shrimp

2 pounds shrimp, shelled
2 tablespoons olive oil
1 large onion, chopped (about 2 cups)
2 stalks celery, sliced
1/4 cup chopped bell pepper
1 cup chopped fresh parsley
4 green onions, chopped (about 1/2 cup)
1/2 cup dry white wine
4 cups chopped tomatoes, canned and drained or fresh
2 cloves garlic, crushed through a press
1 tablespoon Worcestershire sauce
1 cup tomato sauce
1/4 teaspoon salt
1/4 teaspoon thyme
1/8 teaspoon cayenne pepper
1/2 teaspoon dried mint
Cooked rice or noodles

In a large skillet, heat the oil on medium high. Add the onions, celery, bell pepper, parsley, and green onions. Saute until the onions are clear and the peppers are soft.

Stir in the wine, tomatoes, garlic, Worcestershire, tomato sauce, salt, thyme, cayenne pepper and mint. Cover and cook over medium heat until the sauce comes to a boil. Reduce the heat to low and simmer 40 minutes. Add the shrimp and continue simmering 10 minutes more, stirring occasionally. Serve over cooked rice or noodles.

Makes 8 servings.

In traditional versions of this Scandinavian dish, the fish is allowed to cure for several days and eaten raw. In this recipe, the fish is cured in the time-honored way but it's baked and served hot or cold. It's a beautiful appetizer for a holiday party but it's a great entree, too.

Baked Gravlax

1 1/2 pounds fresh salmon fillet, center-cut
2 tablespoons salt
4 teaspoons sugar
1 teaspoon coarsely ground pepper
1 tablespoon brandy
1/4 cup fresh dill or 1 teaspoon dried
Fresh lemon wedges (for garnish)
5 tablespoons capers (for garnish)
Pickled white onions (for garnish)

Combine the salt, sugar and pepper. Rub into fish on all sides. Sprinkle with brandy. Place some of the dill in the bottom of a glass dish. Place the salmon on top. Cover with remaining dill. Wrap dish well with plastic wrap. Allow to marinate overnight or up to 36 hours, checking occasionally. Baste fish with the juices.

Preheat oven to 400 F. When ready to cook, scrape dill and salt coating off fish. Lightly oil a baking dish and cook for 15 to 20 minutes depending on thickness of the fish. Transfer to a platter.

The fish can be served hot or chilled. If served chilled, garnish with lemon, capers and pickled onions.

Makes 4 servings.

Notes: This is excellent with Old Fashioned Tartar Sauce (recipe page 200) or Tarragon Cream Sauce (recipe page 199).

This lasagna only gets better and better after it's made and reheated. It wins big praise at buffet suppers and pot luck dinners.

Crab and Artichoke Lasagna

Non-stick cooking spray

3 sheets fresh lasagna pasta (preferably spinach) or 1 (12-ounce) package ruffled lasagna noodles

1 pound fresh crab meat, picked over to remove cartilage and shell

1 (14-ounce) can artichoke hearts or bottoms, in brine (not marinated in oil)

4 tablespoons butter or margarine

1 medium yellow onion, diced

4 tablespoons all-purpose flour

3/4 teaspoon salt

1/4 teaspoon white pepper

1 (8-ounce) bottle clam juice

1 cup evaporated skim milk

1/4 teaspoon nutmeg

2 tablespoons white wine

2 cloves garlic

1 cup finely chopped fresh parsley or fresh basil

1 (16 ounce) container part-skim ricotta cheese

1/4 cup Parmesan cheese

1 egg white

1 cup part-skim mozzarella cheese

 imitation crab, shrimp, cooked salmon, tuna, lobster

Notes: You can find fresh pasta in Italian delicatessens and some grocery stores. You can substitute peas or blanched asparagus for the artichokes.

Preheat oven to 350 F.

Spray a 9-by-13-inch glass baking dish with non-stick spray. Set aside. Pick over crab to remove any pieces of cartilage or shell; set aside. Drain artichokes and cut into quarters; set aside. In a saucepan, heat the butter or margarine. Stir in the onion and cook for 2 minutes.

Whisk in flour, salt and pepper. Cook for 2 minutes over medium heat, until flour begins to bubble and turn golden brown. Add the clam juice and milk in dribbles, whisking constantly.

Stir constantly and bring to a boil. Mixture will thicken. Simmer for 2 to 3 minutes. Remove from heat and set aside. Stir in nutmeg, wine and crab. In the bowl of a food processor or blender, mince garlic and parsley or basil. Add ricotta, Parmesan and egg white. Puree until fine; set aside. Bring 2 quarts of water to a boil. Trim pasta dough to size of baking dish. If using fresh pasta, cook each sheet in boiling water for 2 minutes. Remove and drain. Continue with each sheet. If using dry pasta, cook according to package directions.

Lay dough in the bottom of the baking dish. Spoon 1/3 of the crab mixture over. Lay half the artichokes on top and cover with 1/3 of the garlic and ricotta mixture. Cover with another sheet of pasta dough. Spread 1/3 of crab mixture on top, and cover with remaining artichokes. Spread with 1/3 of the ricotta mixture. Lay last sheet of pasta dough in pan. Top with remaining crab and ricotta mixtures. Sprinkle with mozzarella.

Bake for 40 minutes. If necessary, place under oven broiler for another 10 minutes to brown the top.

Allow to stand 10 to 15 minutes. Serve with lemon wedges.

Makes 10 servings.

Colorful and indescribably delicious. Don't stop to answer the phone when you make this beautiful dish or the paper-thin dough will dry out. Shop for Middle Eastern phyllo dough in the frozen foods section of most grocery stores.

Spinach and Salmon en Croute

1 pound cooked salmon, flaked

2 (10-ounce) packages frozen spinach, thawed

3 tablespoons butter

4 green onions, chopped

1/2 cup chopped fresh parsley

1 teaspoon dried basil or dill

1/2 teaspoon salt

1/2 teaspoon pepper

1/4 teaspoon nutmeg

1 egg

1 1/2 cups shredded Gruyere or Swiss cheese, divided

1/2 cup (1 stick) unsalted butter, melted and cooled

20 sheets phyllo dough (for best results use 9-by-13-inch sheets)

 crab meat, cooked tuna, cooked shrimp

Notes: For the best results, use the clear, yellow butterfat on the surface of the melted butter and avoid the milky solids at the bottom. The milk solids make the dough soggy and fragile.

If you're in a real hurry, substitute frozen puff pastry for the phyllo dough in this dish. Roll it out very thinly before fitting it in the springform pan because it puffs a lot during baking.

If you can't find fresh salmon, substitute a 16-ounce can of red salmon, drained, with skin and bones discarded.

Check for bones in the salmon. Break into bite-sized pieces and set aside.

Squeeze the excess liquid out of the spinach; it should be fairly dry. Set aside. In a saute pan, heat the butter. When it foams, add the green onions and saute until soft. Remove from heat and stir in the spinach, parsley, basil or dill, salt, pepper, nutmeg, egg and Swiss cheese.

Use a paintbrush or pastry brush to lightly butter the bottom and sides of a 9-inch springform pan. Fit 1 sheet of the phyllo dough in the bottom and up the sides. Brush pastry lightly with melted butter, including the sides. Layer and brush 10 sheets of dough, turning the dish after each sheet so the edges are even all around. Layer half the salmon on the bottom, top with half the spinach mixture, the other half of the salmon and remaining spinach mixture.

Layer 10 sheets of phyllo dough on top of the filling, brushing each lightly with the melted butter. Turn the dish after each sheet so the edges are even all around. When the last sheet has been added, roll the edges of the pastry to make a decorative border.

Use a small sharp knife to lightly score the surface into 8 or 10 even pieces. Do not cut all the way through the pastry. (This makes it easier to cut into serving pieces after baking.) Refrigerate for up to 24 hours before baking.

When ready to bake, preheat oven to 325 F. Bake for 45 minutes or until pastry is golden brown on top. Allow to cool for about 10 minutes before cutting.

Makes 10 servings.

INDEX